WHY ME LORD?

ANNIE DAVID

There has never been any question in my mind as to whom this book should be dedicated to.

To,

My beloved husband David Lucas

Contents

Contents

Contents

About The Book

I am very pleased to write a few words about this captivating book 'Why me Lord?' However, writing about this book surpasses everything, because the author of this book happens to be my beloved wife.

I feel so complete with Annie; and cannot thank God enough for bringing us together in life! The best thing that ever happened in my life is Annie sharing her life with me. I can say this with all my heart. I often tell myself that she is my best half and my heart has been blossoming with love, joy and peace from the moment Annie and I exchanged vows saying 'I do' at the altar.

It has not always been a fairy tale that ended happily, we have had our ups and downs, mountain peak experience as well as tears in the valleys. Annie shares these experiences very vividly here. In all this, it is the strong bond of love between us and our clinging together on to our Lord, that we find our marriage so joyful even today. As a couple, we are committed to the great commission of our Lord. "Go ye into the world making disciples of all nations, in Jerusalem, in Judea, in Samaria and unto the ends of the earth."

David Lucas

About The Author

Annie David who was born in Tamil Nadu, southern India to nominal Christian parents, started writing at the age of 20. Annie was a unique gift from the Lord Jesus to her family. She started working as a teacher in Abu Dhabi for nearly 18 years, after which she followed God's calling to resign her Job and, together with husband and children, returned to India, setting aside her family's dream to emigrate to Canada. She, with her beloved husband, started their own school here, with the motive to serve the poor children of Erachakulam village in Kanniyakumari District in TamilNadu, near her hometown. David and Annie are blessed with three children; Angelina, Adlien and Joshua.

This book is a powerful testimony of her personal life that she shares with grace. It is hoped that this work of Annie David will inspire and encourage the readers and challenge them to full dependence on Christ, who so marvellously worked His plan for her life.

Acknowledgements

I was inspired, directed and energised by the Holy Spirit during the entire preparation of this book.

The prayer support given me by several God's people is highly appreciated. I am greatly indebted to my precious husband David Lucas for his willing help in numerous areas without which this book would not have become a reality.

I greatly appreciate the assistance of our children during the writing of the manuscript. Our first daughter Angelina has been very instrumental during the writing of the book. Our second daughter Adlien designed the beautiful cover of the book. Our son Joshua read through the first draft and made the basic corrections. My friend Mrs Janie Garrett gave some valuable comments on the manuscript. Dr Robert B Grubh edited the entire manuscript and also did the initial page formatting of the book.

Preface

I love to see people succeed with their life - so does God, the Creator. As the artist treasures his painting and the master craftsman the quality of the violin he created, so does our maker cherish the dreams, goals, excellence of life and the happiness you and I are to enjoy on this earth and beyond. The boundaries and benchmarks of Christian living are often obscured by human wisdom based on one's personal opinions and preconceived notions. It is a gross mistake. You and I are not a law unto ourselves. We have a definite yardstick by which our spiritual and moral stature should be measured. That yardstick is the Lord Jesus. 'Am I like Him?' is the only question that we need to ask ourselves, 'Do I think and talk and act as the Lord Jesus did?' should be our chief concern.

The clock of eternity is fast approaching the midnight hour. Lawlessness abounds around us. We have been too slow to open our blind eyes, so that they can distinguish light from darkness. The squalid depths of immorality are looked upon as high fashion and even the stream of justice is often polluted by greed, avarice and an inability to discern right from wrong.What about those whose lives are filled with regret? What about those who have committed gross sins? Or those who are trapped into meaningless marriage? Where do such people begin their quest for peace and fulfilment?

My conviction is that failure of some kind is common to us all. And since God had people like us in mind when Christ made the supreme sacrifice, God's grace is adequate to help us make the best of any situation. Successful people are those who apply God's remedy for their failure.

This book has been written with the earnest prayer that it might be an encouragement to us as Christians. As I shall explain later, some people believe that their successes may actually be failures; others who have failed may really be quite successful. For all, there is hope. Salvation was designed for people who have made mistakes, failed and sinned. Despite our past, all of us can say, 'I delight to do Thy will, O my God' (Psalms 40:8).

Do these words reflect your experience and echo your plea as a believer? Do you sometimes feel hemmed in by the world, the flesh and the devil to the point that you wonder if your Christianity is worth anything? Do you sometimes fear that you will never be all that God called you to be? Do you long to get on with your Christian maturity and experience the freedom, which God's word promises?

I want to share my hope with you in the pages ahead. Your maturity is the product of time, pressure, trials, tribulations, the knowledge of God's word, an understanding of who you are in Christ, and the presence of the Holy Spirit in your life. You probably already have the first four elements in abundance; most Christians do. Stir them together well and then watch yourself begin to grow!

I pray that this book may enrich the lives of those who read it with an open heart, and release in them the spirit of worship abundantly. Read it with expectation and receive great rewards. You will hear the clear voice of the Holy Spirit in your heart. You will experience the immeasurable power of worship in your lives. May the good Lord bless you through this book.

Annie David

Foreword

"'And I will make thee a great nation, and I will bless thee, and make thy name great; and thou shalt be a blessing'(Genesis 12: 2)."

The person, whom I know to secure this verse in her life as a promise of God is Mrs. Anne David. She was my Sunday school teacher and my mentor who helped me to develop my skills in many aspects in my childhood. She also made a great impact in my life during my formative years. God's wonderful ways of working are evident through her life.

Life is not always a bed of roses. Difficulties are always there to test us. How God wonderfully walked with her throughout life's struggles is depicted in this book, to encourage the readers to understand the incomprehensible and incomparable ways of God. This book helps the readers to enrich their faith in God and also encourages them to possess the fruit of the Spirit.

Although she was the daughter of a medical doctor, she chose her mother's occupation, teaching. Leaving her affluent life in Abu Dhabi, she chose to do the will of God by teaching the downtrodden of village Erachakulam. Along with the teaching, students have been imparted the love of God for twenty years.

Accepting the challenges is one of the greatest skills which one can develop upon the love of God. The experiences, which she gained by the challenges she faced while being a student, friend, wife, mother and teacher, made her submit herself to God's perfect will to see His wonderful guidance. And those experiences of her, mentioned in this book, will definitely be a take away for the readers.

One might have felt bad about how women are not equally treated as men in their own homes, society and also in the church in our area. On the contrary, women are so special in the eyes of God and deserving to receive the blessings from our Lord as it is evident throughout her life. Thus, her experiences give life to her writings. The ups and downs of life will determine the development in one's character such as love, tolerance, acceptance, humility and faith. It helps everyone who reads this book to understand the purpose of life and brings blessings.

May the Lord give us greater faith and a greater spiritual boldness to pray stupendous prayer; asking God for great things, things that only He can do.

Let God help everyone who reads this book to take part in the revival of our nation.

Dr. Jane Katherin Ruskin M.Sc., M.Ed., Ph.D.,
Principal, Belfield Matric Hr. Sec. School,
Asaripallam - 629 201

Epigraph

CHAPTER ONE

Introduction

I found myself uprooted and replanted from Abu Dhabi UAE to this remote village in the southern tip of India in the year of 2001. This shift was possible by the divine will and plan of God alone. I would say we were taken out from the comfort zone and from a familiar place into an unfamiliar place with new people. We came to be in this place of new beginnings. I began to experience the fellowship of my Lord Jesus Christ anew.

My husband David was working for an oil company in Abu Dhabi and I was teaching in the Abu Dhabi Indian School. Our daughters were fourteen and thirteen years of age and our son was ten years then. Our children were studying in the same school where I was working. At that time we were considering emigrating to Canada to give our children a better education and opportunities. However, the turn of events directed the five of us as a family to come back to South India to start a primary school in a remote village called Erachakulam.

During this period, having quiet time with the Lord meant a lot to me. No availability of the Internet in those days was in fact a great opportunity to spend more quality time with the Lord and be led to walk with the Lord; holding on to His word and His grace alone. This great source of divine help took us through situations of loneliness, hardships and the unfamiliar and unknown future.

We built our lives together, trusting in the provisions and hope of our Lord even as we went to serve the village community in southern India; and we continue to grow each day. This story has evolved from a series of my quiet times with the Lord and of Bible devotions I had been dwelling on to draw my strength from. These wonderful truths of God have drawn me closer to my God day after day for two long decades in this village.

The leading of the Holy Spirit and the gentle shepherding of our master shepherd has always guided us and taken us in the paths of righteousness. I would like to share with you my life experiences with the hope and desire that this piece of work may encourage all of you, readers, to see the master plan of God in your own lives too. Trust me, you will be amazed how blessed you are when you decide to hold hands with Jesus as you walk through life's narrow path. Today we stand as a testimony of God's unfailing love and power.

CHAPTER TWO

A Vivid Dream

I wonder how much of those childhood memories anyone could remember late into adult life. In all of my life, a particular dream I had very early in life was very significant. It is fresh in my memory and I can even now recollect it as if I saw it yesterday. In a way, my Lord has been tugging at my reins all these past years to take me to the ultimate destination, and this dream was a foretaste of His divine plan for my life.

I was about four years old when this incident happened. I was standing one evening near the rear gate of the compound wall of our home in my village Paloor near Karungal in Kanniyakumari district, Tamil Nadu in southern India. From this gate I could have a good view of the villagers rushing to buy oil for their lamps, groceries, heading to the fish market etc. While I stood there, a young man who had a sling bag made of cloth over his shoulder and had a bunch of tracts in his hand. He handed me one which bore the pictorial explanation of both hell and heaven.

I took it home and gave it to my Grandma (whose name was also Annie). She sat me on her lap and showed me the pictures and began to explain the picture of a happy face overlooking a pure heart with a rejoicing angel and the devil having no place in the heart. There was another picture with a sad face overlooking a heart within which were tiny shapes of a snake, a lion, peacock, frog, tortoise, pig, and a goat, each depicting human nature such as pride, anger, ferocity and so on, she said. She also explained how heaven is a good place to be in, which is filled with joy and light. And that hell is a place of pain, eternal fire and worms. There was another picture on the back side of the tract, a picture of a road that forked out into two pathways. One was leading to a dark and gloomy place (hell). People who were going towards hell were carrying a heavy burden on which was written sin, their faces were gloomy and dark. The other path led to a place filled with angels and bright lights, and people were rejoicing on this pathway. It took a while to process all that I had seen in those pictures after asking many questions.

I finally went to bed that night with these thoughts still in my mind, and I had a vivid dream. I dreamt of the last picture on the tract. I saw people walking down to the dark, gloomy, scary place called hell with a big sack on their backs, and I also saw people walking up to heaven rejoicing along the way. I then saw myself at the fork, and I was unsure of which path to choose. This decision was mine alone to make since it was just me standing there as I was unable to decide which way to choose at that time. I saw people climbing the uphill pathway and many were happily and joyfully going to a place of light shining ever so bright, which I cannot explain.

Yet there were also many with tears of anguish and agony heading towards the dirty, dark place where there was wailing, weeping and terribly fearsome loud tormenting noise. I was terrified by what I saw. It was then that I woke up and began to sob in bitter tears in the darkness of the night, as there was no electricity in our village at that time, there was a small lamp burning in the bedroom. In the silence of the night I woke up my mother, told her my dream and asked her just one question, 'Which path to choose, the one to heaven or hell?' She plainly replied, 'Go to heaven' and went back to sleep. I knew that I didn't want to go to hell; I also knew that I did not deserve to go to heaven. Many years later, I realized I had to ask for forgiveness. Things I saw in the dream are so vivid that even the passing of years could not erase it from my mind. In the later years I had to deal with this cross-road challenge. I will share more about this in later chapters.

CHAPTER THREE

My Family

My paternal grandparents are Isaac and Annie. Grandpa started his ministry as an evangelist in the year 1900. Grandpa and Grandma had six children, and the youngest was Wilson, my Papa. My maternal grandfather was Dr Sundramony and my maternal grandmother, Ponabarna. Grandpa was working in Munnar tea estate in a hospital as a doctor in the early years of 1920. Munnar means three rivers in both Tamil and Malayalam languages. As the word denotes, it is located at the confluence of three mountain streams. Most of the population there consisted of workers of the tea plantations.

My mother was the oldest in the family of three brothers and three sisters. I have pleasant memories of my visit to her home in Munnar during my annual holidays while I wa in primary school. When I think of my stay with my maternal grandparents in Munnar, my memories are so green even today. I can recall the chillness of the weather, the lovely meadows and the ride on Grandpa's horse. Above all, the sweet fragrance of the lovely roses in the gardens and the wild roses growing in the unused lands; the healthy cows grazing on the green meadows, the smoke from the home kitchens, most of all I cannot forget the steam engine train journey winding up and down the hilly Munnar rail tracks and the huffing sound of smoke and exhaust gas. The train whistle was originally referred to as a steam trumpet, an audible signalling device on a steam locomotive used to warn of an approaching train. The sight and the experience are still a wonder, and what a power these memories still carry, I am amazed.

My father, Dr Wilson, studied to become a male nurse and had worked in Aramco Saudi from 1944 to 1950. He later returned to India and went to the Osmania Medical College in Hyderabad and became a qualified doctor himself. He started practicing as a private medical practitioner in our village, Paloor, living in the family home with my grandparents.

It so happened that my oldest uncle from my father's side was the headmaster of the only High School in Munnar then, he was also the senior Maths teacher. My mother and her siblings went to this high school and I heard them talk about their strict Headmaster Mr Russel. My mother, Bellage Helen was one of his students in the final school year; and she always stood first in her class. As the academic year was ending, Mr Russel thought to himself that his student Helen would be the apt match for his youngest brother Wilson, As per the traditions he initiated the proposal for his brother. The elders of both families met and arranged to see the bride and the groom. Eventually the wedding took place in 1952 in Chenamvilai which is my maternal grandparents' village in Kanniyakumari district. My parents settled in Paloor in the family home with my father's parents who lived in a joint family set up. I was born to my parents and grew up in this family home.

My Papa had his clinic set up in the front room next to the hall of our home where the outpatients were examined and treated. We, children, were not allowed to go to the front room of our own house or even to the hall! I saw two big wooden cupboards in which were kept different kinds of medicines and other medical supplies. The patients and their attendees would sit on the wooden benches and Papa would ask for their complaints and then examine them with his stethoscope.

He would then measure different medicines in his ounce glass and fill them into a bottle for fever, cough, flu and so on as needed. I saw him sterilizing the injection needles in his small spirit lamp before using it on a patient. If the patient happened to be a child we could hear piercing screams. In those days most of the patients in our village did not pay their fees to the doctor by cash. Instead, they brought chicken, chicken eggs, bananas, jackfruit, coconut, cashewnut, and lentils. The patients from coastal areas would even bring fresh fish.

Almost every day, there was someone in his clinic irrespective of the hour of the day or night. I used to witness men coming at midnight with hurricane lanterns or fire torches made of coconut tree leaves braided together, unlike the modern torch lights. My father used to go with these men to attend emergency cases such as delivery of a baby or sometimes accidents. There was no electricity in those days in our village until the early 1960's. At home we used kerosene lamps. At times my father would also refer some cases to doctors in the cities nearby.

Proper health care was needed to manage diseases, reduce treatable disabilities and premature deaths. Learning from all these health problems around me in those early years of my life, I resolved to become a physician myself in order to help the women and children in the community.

My mother, Bellage Helen, started teaching in a government school soon after she completed her secondary school teachers training program. She used to be an exceptional teacher. She was presented by the Governor of Tamil Nadu the prestigious 'Best Teacher Award' for the year 1988 for teachers of Tamil Nadu government schools. The award included a merit certificate, a cash award and a medal.

My Amma was also known for her creative works. I used to admire her a lot. My Amma was a very industrious woman. She would hand-stitch all my clothes, as she never had a sewing machine until later in life. She used to make my frocks, dresses, embroidery wall hangings and all sorts of decorations. She also took an active part in church activities, especially in Sunday school. She was also responsible for all women's church projects. She used to be a fun-loving person. In those days women in the village, if they had any disputes, would come to my mother for mediation; so she was nicknamed a 'village magistrate'.

Joint family had been a traditional practice in those days and our family was no exception. In a joint family, the daughter-in-law of the house is responsible for the running of the entire house, especially cooking, housekeeping and caring for the old. Soon after her marriage my mother was given these joint family responsibilities and this continued until late 1975 when my aunt left the family house to a place of her own. A little later my uncle, too left, but my mother cared for all of them - even my Grandma and Grandpa - till the end of their days. Doing her best to the Lord and for her family, she entered eternity at the age of seventy.

Grandma was an easy going fun loving young woman from a wealthy family. Her father was a doctor. Her parents arranged for her to marry an evangelist, Isaac. Becoming the wife of an evangelist was a sudden shift from the life she was used to. Adjusting and adapting to this new life was not easy. My Grandpa was working under the South Indian United Church, which later in 1947 came to be called CSI, the Church of South India.

My Grandpa Isaac was a man of few words and I was told that he used to spend a lot of time studying the word of God. He was among the learned men of the society at that time as he had passed Sixth Form, which then gave him the right to be in a position to join the university. He was able to converse fluently in English to the British people around us in the pre-Independence days. Grandma had learnt to read and write Tamil and English, as I recollect now.

Those days were known for severe scarcity of water in our part of India, and people went walking at least a couple of kilometres to find ponds, rivers or fresh springs to bathe in and to carry back drinking water. It was my Grandma's practice to go with neighbouring ladies for this morning chore. During these long walks they exchanged stories and events and incidents.

Typically, on one particular day a story intrigued my Grandma as one of her friends shared to the group how she happened to steal money from her husband. The women of those days never worked to earn money. Hearing this, other ladies also added their bit to it, and as my Grandma listened to them, she came up with an idea to do the same experiment with my Grandpa too. So coming home that day, Grandma chose a time when her husband was not at home and stole a chakaram (coin) from the one and only coat he had and kept it with her.

When the evening came, Grandpa went into his room to pray as usual and it took some time for him to come out. Being curious, Grandma just went to his room where the door was partly closed and she overheard the sobbing cry as he pleaded with God for the one missing chakram he had kept in his coat pocket for his family needs. Hearing this, Grandma was so convicted and returned the chakram back to him and asked for forgiveness.

In 1919 Grandma Annie had a life changing experience right after her sixth child, Wilson, was born, her life suddenly left her body. It was said that her body was cold and that she was not breathing. Her baby was lying next to her 'lifeless' body. Nobody knew what had happened till she awoke after a few hours from her deep 'sleep' and was frantically looking for her baby boy. She then sat up and told her family the unspeakable experience she had in the heavenly home above.

An angel took her, she said, to heaven where seated on a majestic throne was Jesus. Bright light filled this marvelous place and there were numerous angels around. Then Jesus called her name, and she was ushered into His presence where she was given a tour by Jesus Himself of the different homes Jesus was preparing for those who are going to be in heaven one day; and she was shown where her home was in progress, and then she saw the crystal clear living waters and the lovely garden of flowers of different colours and fragrance. Then she saw a garden where countless trees were loaded with fruits of different varieties. She continued to walk the streets of gold, where people of all ages filled the place with unending joy, and my Grandma was lost in that place of peace and joy.

There was a silence all of a sudden and she looked deeply into the face of Jesus and noticed tears of pain and the next moment she saw deep down a valley from where tormenting cries arose from an agonizing place called hell. But she was held close to Jesus' bosom and Jesus asked her in a sorrowful voice: 'Will you go back and tell my people around you and your family to accept the love I have for each one of them to keep them away from this place?' Grandma said 'Yes' but also added, 'I don't want to go back.' She pleaded with Jesus to keep her in heaven, but Jesus sternly told her 'Annie, just look down from here', she looked down and saw her baby boy lying next to her lifeless body. She was then asked to go back to raise her son and bring many into the saving grace of Jesus. From then on she continued to serve God along with Grandpa as she lived for 44 more years and entered her glorious home in 1963, when I was ten years of age.

I am the oldest of five children in our family, I have three younger sisters and one brother. The sister next to me is Pon Malar Christabel, also known as Jiji.

Next was my sister Nirmala Grace (Suji), a very loving, hardworking and strong-willed woman. Her daughter is married and settled in the U.A.E and her son is pursuing Media and Communication. Sadly, she has passed on to her glorious home.

Next is my only brother Isaac Sundersen, also known as Suresh. He studied to be a doctor and specialized in Orthopaedics. I am very proud of what my brother has become, in fact my dream to become a doctor in order to be of service to the community was fulfilled by God in my brother being used for this purpose, to be the hands that touch and heal. Many young and old from all over India, even people from other nations like Dubai, Maldives and Muscat have come to him for treatment. He has a son and a daughter who are also pursuing medicine.

The youngest among all of us is my sister Jiji Malar Christabel, also known as Jeena. Jeena is a teacher by profession who did her post-graduation in Botany and did her M.Ed as well. She has two boys who are pursuing Engineering.

Growing up, we enjoyed each other's company during our childhood days. We used to play together but only within the compound as we were not allowed to go outside. Being restricted this way, we enjoyed the company of each other. As we were not allowed to go outside, we did not have any friends from the village.

Jiji used to share with me some of the exceptional dreams she used to have about glimpses of heaven and the experience of singing melodious songs with the angels. She used to try to explain the visions of heaven that she had, but I never paid much attention, nor did I ask for any details.

CHAPTER FOUR

LIFE IN MY VILLAGE

As mentioned earlier, water scarcity was a challenge in those days. We had to fetch drinking water from a well which was nearly a kilometre away from the village, and the water had to be rationed like two to three pots per family during summers. Drinking water was stored in earthen pots. For the bathing and washing of clothes we sometimes walked for about two to three kilometres to find a pond or a spring with fresh water. Those days as children, my cousins accompanied our aunts and walked this distance to wash the family clothes and partially dry them nearby in a dry place where there was grass and then carry it home as it was easier to carry than wet clothes. Usually the regime of the family laundry was once a week. My aunt would dry clothes on a clothesline in the backyard, where there was a haystack for the cows, a stack of firewood, a cow shed for two cows and calves, a goat shed beside it and a chicken coop.

I remember receiving a harmonica from a family member, I treasured it as a priceless gift. As far as I can remember I had not received any gift before that I valued this much. I taught myself to play this musical instrument and within a few months I could play a few Sunday school songs. My parents were not used to the sound of musical instruments and would often get irritated with the sound of me playing. Being thrilled with this newly acquired talent of mine, I used to play the harmonica for long hours.

I cannot forget this particular event one day with my harmonica. I climbed to the top of a guava tree in our backyard and got comfortable before I started playing. The music could be heard all over the area. To my horror, as I was enthralled in playing my harmonica, I suddenly saw the angry face of my Papa, holding his walking stick standing right under the tree! I attempted to climb down hurriedly, but sadly my skirt got stuck in a branch and I found myself hanging upside down from one of the branches.

Fear and shame enveloped me as I was soon surrounded by my cousins and family. Nothing and nobody could save me from my Papa's wrath that day.

In a day with a variety of toys and gadgets both electronic and of various other forms, my mind often takes me back to my childhood where I was playing in the backyard of our home with coconut shells, sticks, dirt, sand, mud, dry leaves, flowers and water, playing with kitchen toys, cooking or pretending to be a teacher in a classroom with my other cousins around. I don't remember if any of us had any other toys to play with. My cousin's brothers used to play with bicycle tires to roll and run behind. They also rolled up rags to replicate a football and played with it.

Observing the Sabbath in the 1960s under our grandparents' leadership was extremely special and rigid. Sunday meals were cooked by Grandma the previous day, we never cooked on Sundays. The firewood was not lit in the kitchen; and there was no sight of smoke coming out of the kitchen chimney. Those days in churches we had Sunday services both in the morning as well as in the evening. In addition, we had Sunday school, youth meetings, Christian endeavour and women's fellowship. So Grandma and Grandpa mostly stayed back in the church. As children, we never did any work other than staying at home and singing songs, reading the scriptures and resting only if we wanted to, even when we had tests or exams the next day. Even my own children followed the same Sunday routine. Even visiting or entertaining friends or relatives are avoided.

In this, we follow the Lord's command, which says in Isaiah 58:13-14, 'If you turn away your foot from the Sabbath, from doing your pleasure on My holy day, and call the Sabbath a delight, the holy day of the Lord honourable, and shall honour Him, not doing your own ways, nor finding your own pleasure, nor speaking your own words, then you shall delight yourself in the Lord; and I will cause you to ride on the high hills of the earth, and feed you with the heritage of Jacob your father. The mouth of the Lord has spoken.'

In those days when telephone facilities were non-existent, we used to have unannounced guests. For example, my maternal uncle and his family along with three children once visited us all of a sudden; and that too around lunch time! Since they were coming from far, they had to start their journey very early in the morning, partly walking and catching two or three buses from Pothencode in Kerala, which is about 90 km from our village. It was a very interesting experience and the responsibility of our family is to prepare lunch for them. We needed to cook chicken since we had some roosters at home. The challenge was to catch one of them as they have already been let out from the coop into the open compound. We all would team up and try to corner one rooster, but sometimes it would escape into the neighbour's yard. So we took help from the neighbouring kids to catch this rooster and bring it home.

The height of the meal preparation was grinding the masala for the curry, which was my personal responsibility. Sitting down at the grinding stone called ammikkal, and grinding the spices was an unavoidable pain those days. Ammikkal consisted of two parts: a solid rectangular stone and an enormous stone rolling pin called ammikkozhavi. Both had pitted surface which helped in grinding the spices and scraped coconut.

The ammikkozhavi is repeatedly drawn against the ammikkal with the spices in between, which in the process get crushed and become a fine paste. This masala paste is then added to the chicken and cooked. The reign of ammikkal ended when the electric mixer grinder came to the market later in the 20th century. Since the advent of the mixer grinder or 'mixie', as it was affectionately called, the ammikkal and ammikkozhavi went to rest in the attic.

My Amma would then use the finely ground masala to prepare the chicken which was shared with our guests and we all loved it. Such meals with guests used to be a memorable family affair those days.

Our grandparents and elders in the family had a practice of eating a piece of palm jaggery known in Tamil as karuppukkatti shortened karupatti after meals. On hot summer days, people would eat a piece of karupatti and drink water. If we have any workers in our land, it was a practice to offer them this karupatti and water from a chembu (copper vessel).

Now let me say a few words about the preparation of karupatti. Palm juice is first extracted from Palmyra trees, which were plentiful in our neighbourhood. Specialised Palmyra climbers would first gently scrape the outer coating of Palmira flowers. This induces slow dripping of the palm juice, which gets collected in small earthen pots tied overnight below the flowers, and brought down in the morning. A tiny bit of pure lime (Calcium hydroxide) or chunnambu is immediately added by the climbers in order to prevent it from fermenting. This sweet drink is called pathaneer in Tamil and neera in Hindi. If chunnambu is not added immediately, the juice would start fermenting fast and become an intoxicating drink called toddy, or kallu in Tamil.

Growing up at home, the boiling of this palm juice to make karupatti was a regular regime. The pathaneer is boiled for two to three hours to remove the water content and then the thick liquid is poured into coconut shells in which it solidifies into yellowish brown karupatti. My Grandma poured water over the leftover syrup in the vessel and boiled it with some coffee powder or tea leaves and served it as Karupatti Kappi. I am not kidding you, this was probably the most unique and best tasting beverage I have ever had in those days, the taste still lingers on in my tongue. Those days, the entire house would smell of this aromatic jaggery. The labourer who climbs these trees would have the palm juice every other day as his wages.

CHAPTER FIVE

My Life Takes A Major Turn

When I was 9 years old, my father decided to enroll me in the 6th grade in an English medium school which was in Nagercoil, a city located about 40 km away from my village. I don't think he consulted my mother or me on the matter. This was indeed a great change for me mainly because I was not at all prepared mentally, physically and intellectually. If only my father had prepared me for this big change I would have done well in my class, coming to think of it now. But I had no choice, and if I had refused, I knew what to expect from my father with his dictator mind set. My dear mother as usual adhered to his decisions.

One fine day, my suitcase was packed and I was dropped off at Duthie Boarding School the very next day. I felt so lonely, helpless and sad. I was like a fish out of water most of the time, I felt homesick with the sudden transition and separation from home. I was very badly affected by this drastic change and expectations of campus life in a sophisticated city. I had a decrease in appetite because of my inadequacy to handle the new environment. Preoccupying thoughts of my home and attachment to my familiarity and objects tormented me. With the withdrawn behaviour and difficulty in focusing on everything unrelated to home, there was a feeling of stress and anxiety. I just needed love, protection and security, the feelings and qualities associated with home.

I had no role model, no one to look up to, no not one. When evening came, the hostel warden, Mrs. John, who was elderly and kind looking, with white curly hair, called us all for a meeting and gave us several instructions about various timings, rules and regulations. The total number of students of the boarding school was about 100, from 6th grade to 11th grade and ranging in age from 10 to 16. I was the youngest of them all.

The next day I was given instructions to be ready for my first day of school in the 6th grade. My class teacher Mrs. Jazzy started off with the solar system, names of planets and so on, all in English. The next was the science class, where vitamin A to E deficiency diseases, symptoms etc. were taught. Everything was taught in English and not in Tamil! I had just come out of 5th grade in my village school where I had only learnt to read and write the first 3 alphabets of the English language. I found myself totally lost; and I could not make out the head or tail of what was being taught. I questioned, 'was this the case only for me?' In my life everything seemed to be different, with having no friends and no sympathy. Everything seemed to be hard to cope with and I began to dread each new day.

In boarding school I could not cope with the routine, as my level of understanding and motivation was not up to the school standard. The lessons were very hard for me to grasp. I began to fall sick frequently and was taken to the sick room where I had to stay all alone. At fixed times during the day, the kitchen staff would come to check on me and bring me medicine and food. Physically and emotionally I was challenged for the first time in my life. I used to cry in silence almost every day, mostly because I missed my home. In that sick room, in the darkness of the night I remember sobbing many times with bitter tears.

At the end of the academic year, my father was called in by the school Principal, Miss. Mathew who explained the difficulties I faced in the school as well as in the hostel; my inability to cope with the subjects in the school was a prime concern. She explained that I would need to repeat the same grade the next year as well. My father took me home that weekend and he asked me if I would like to switch from Duthie School and attend the school back in my village. My parents, seeing my state of mind, and my tears, gave me an option to come back from this elite private school and resume my studies in the village Government High school near my village.

This option seemed good, apparently since all the teachers in this school were my mother's ex-students and she too continued to work as a senior teacher there. As my father was a reputed medical Doctor in the village, our parents were well known in the community. Most of the teachers at the village Government school were well known to my parents and I would have received royal treatment. However, for an unknown reason, I refused this obvious option. I decided to stay on in Duthie School and continue my education there.

I eventually started doing better academically and since I was in a boarding school, I could also take an active interest in sports and games in my free time. I took part in netball and tennikoit and I was even selected to represent our school in inter-school competitions. I won championships, shields, medals, trophies and merit certificates which was an honour and pride for my school. I successfully completed my high school in this English medium school with top grades.

Looking back now, had I chosen to return to my village for my schooling, I would never have learnt and accomplished what I needed to, I would never have become the person I am today. God is still working on me to make me what I ought to be.

I also recollect the following incident that happened when I was in the 9th grade, I was 14 years old at that time. My uncle gifted me a gold ring and I wore it while I was in my boarding school. My bed was in the corner of the dormitory. One night, before bedtime, I removed the ring and kept it beside my bed. The next morning, when I looked for the ring, it was not there. I was very sad and fearful about how my father would react in front of the students and warden of the school hostel, if he found out that I lost the ring.

It was a practice at the boarding school that parents or guardians of the hostel inmates would come to visit every weekend with snacks and goodies during the visiting hours. For weeks my father never noticed my ring not being there on my finger. I prayed almost every day to find my ring. You won't believe it, after three long months of praying and hoping, I found my ring in the very same place I left it, in that very corner. It still remains a mystery as to how God preserved my ring all those months in the very same place I had put it. Praise God for His mercies

CHAPTER SIX

Status Of Girls In The Family

The defining factor which separates a boy from a girl is viewed in those days through the lens of economic gain or otherwise. The village community I hail from, sadly, had a narrow mind-set, which treated boys to be superior to girls. I have researched this and sadly the facts that surfaced were the harsh reality of the system that existed and continues to exist even now. The roles of females, however indispensable, do not attract tangible revenue, whilst the male counterparts are seen having greater earning potential through work and also through receiving hefty dowry from the girl's parents through marriage. Girls are not seen to earn cash or other tradable commodities, but only seen to subtract from the sum total of household income.

Thus, in measuring a female human with a monetary yardstick, her value as a human being is negated and stripped to that of a commodity or asset, devaluing daughters and daughters-in-law as lesser beings.

One must be wondering what happened to the well-known tradition of half saree worn by the junior teen girls. It is mostly forgotten these days. Half saree or thaavani is nothing but a short saree or shawl worn over a long blouse and long skirt or pavaadai, all colour-matched. Wearing a half saree by girls who have come of age was a sign that she is now eligible for marriage.

CHAPTER SEVEN

MY DREAM PLAN VERSUS MY RELATIONSHIP WITH MY FATHER

I had two dream plans for my career. Plan A was to become a medical doctor just like my father, and if not, at least become a nurse. My plan B was to learn advanced English language and do my masters and doctorate in English. To my dismay, my father did not like nor approve either of my plans. So I safely resigned myself to being drifted away with my father's plan. After my schooling I was sent in for a year of Pre-University College (PUC). I was then expected to pursue a Bachelor of Science. So I enrolled in the Women's Christian College in Nagercoil for PUC in the year 1971 and thereafter, for three years a Bachelor's Degree in Zoology at Scott Christian College in the same city.

In Zoology, I had to study animal kingdom including anatomy, embryology, taxonomy, habits and distribution of all animals, both living and some extinct species. I also had to study how these animals fit in their ecosystems. The course also included dissection of frogs, rats, sharks etc. for the study of anatomy. I had to spend many hours of hard work and I did not understand why I needed to undergo all this.

However, the college also had competitions in athletics and games and I was selected to play tennikoit for both singles and doubles. I travelled to other districts to compete in inter-college tournaments. I was the winner of the finals and brought laurels for my college through shields, medals and certificates. The college Principal was very happy with me for this.

No matter how hard I worked to bring my father good marks from school, and tried my best to please him, I simply could not get his appreciation. Whenever I saw fathers openly expressing love towards their daughters in so many ways, I used to crave for such love and admiration from my father. When fathers show love towards their daughters, I believe their self-esteem is enhanced and they can really feel their worth and value in the society they live in.

In fact, in Sunday school, when I was taught that Jesus was our heavenly father, I struggled to understand it and always felt like it was someone else's story. As a result, I could never identify with the love of my father. Growing up, I could understand the essence of fatherhood only when I came to personally know my heavenly Father. Thank God, He never deprived me of the lavish love, which he has poured upon me. He saved the best for me as I am the beloved daughter of the most high God; and I lack nothing.

CHAPTER EIGHT

FACING THE B.SC FINAL EXAM

It was the year 1972, and Christmas was just ending when Jiji turned 12 years old. I was pursuing B.Sc at the time, and I had come home for the holidays. Jiji's birthday was such a great and memorable time that we spent together. Amma had made a delicious biryani that day, but oddly enough, later in the day I began to have a strange feeling.

Jiji tidied up all her belongings that weekend, we arranged our books and other things at our home as if going on a long journey. It did not make any sense to me then, but she gave away all the extras out of her belongings like clothes, books and so on. She gave away a few of her Christmas gifts too. I never questioned her actions, but I did help her with giving away her belongings to the needy village children. It was a family rule that each Sunday we were to memorize a scripture verse which we both did from Psalm 34 that Sunday after church. After spending most of the day singing the Sunday school songs, I boarded the bus to college on Sunday evening.

The following week, on Monday, Jiji developed fever and a headache. As evening approached, on January 5, she became very sick with fever and began to sing songs of heaven and about going to be with Jesus and so on. But none of these made any sense to my mother or to my family. My mother asked her if she was ok. But she replied very clearly that she was happy, and that she was seeing Jesus and she also said to mother, 'Please Amma don't cry; your tears make me sad'. She added: "I am happy, I see Jesus standing there to take me home." My father rushed her to the hospital, but all in vain. After a couple of hours she closed her eyes and never opened them again. She developed meningitis and had been experiencing fever, body pain, and headache. There was inflammation of the protective membranes covering the brain and spinal cord.

My family sent word to me in college, and by the time I reached home, my sister had passed away. I realized that day that life is short and transient, I was left with many questions about life after death. She didn't live any longer to share more of her dreams with me; she had gone to be with the Lord. Little did I know that the week I spent at home with her were her last days on the earth and the Lord was taking her to be with Him forever! Had I known that I would have listened to her experiences and given her more of my attention and time.

Right after the untimely death of our Jiji, my mother was deeply grieved. God, who is close to the broken hearted person, was her only comfort. I have come to realize that every pain that God allows in our lives, has a definite reason behind it. As my mother was grieving over the death of Jiji, she became bedridden for weeks. She had a unique dream which gave her a fresh outlook to this painful memory of her daughter who just died. The dream was like this: My mother was standing in a rose garden looking at the beautiful flowers. Her eyes were drawn to one particular lovely rose when suddenly a hand appeared and plucked that very rose. She began to ask that person why did you pluck that beautiful rose? The hand that appeared turned out to be the hand of the gardener, he said "I need this rose for myself because I am the gardener." There ended her dream; and my mother began to release my sister into the hand of the Gardener, the Maker of this universe who has an ultimate plan for earth and heaven, His ways are past finding. A great peace filled her heart and mind for all the rest of her lifetime. After Jiji passed away, my parents gave her name to my youngest sister who was just six months old then.

It was examination time and I could not focus on my studies well. Those were the challenging times I encountered again of sleepless nights with the thought of my sister, wondering where she had gone, as her loss weighed so heavy on me. I was wrestling in my spirit. I could not be at rest, thinking of my home, now that I was in my hostel room. My mind was with my parents and my siblings with all that was going on at the home front. Finally I managed to complete the course, but only with a low grade. Whenever I recollect my past memories, an element of outstanding truth runs all through my life situations like a fine dark thread all over the fabric of my life events. I never got to hold the reins of my life and to have control over my life situations at any stage.

About this, I used to ask questions and wonder within myself. Whenever I looked around and compared myself with others, I used to get the feeling that the world is not fair to me.

I was deliberately destined to undergo even bitter, painful experiences. Many times I was unable to get out of these painful situations using my own wisdom. I used to think of myself as being trapped. Looking at many others around me being able to make their own life choices and apparently enjoying their life.

As time passed, I started to understand the truth behind all my good and bad experiences in life that 'All things work together for good for those who love the Lord' (Romans 8:28)

CHAPTER NINE

Coming Into God's Family

The Lord never wastes any pain in our lives. I had never considered myself to be a sinner and never thought that I needed the forgiveness of Jesus. I used to have the kind of mind-set that I was a good person. I thought of myself to be a good person since I used to regularly attend church services. Having a good reputation in my college, I used to take pride in the good works my elders and my ancestors had accomplished. I had pride and overconfidence built within me. Reading the book of Sadhu Sunder Singh, also known as the Apostle of the bleeding feet, brought to my mind the dream, which I had when I was about four years old. My puzzled mind began to wonder and be more urgent about finding this hope of eternity.

The wonderful experience my sister used to share with me before she went to be with the Lord, her dreams about heaven, never stirred my spirit in those days. Her vivid description of heavenly angels singing and playing with her never made any sense to me then. However, I do recollect the peace and joy she displayed in her life when she was only 12 years of age.

Now, thoughts began to trouble me that I have no hope of eternity. So I was determined to find a solution to this dilemma which was getting stronger and more disturbing. I could think of no better way than fasting for the first time in my life for the next three days in order to find a solution to the ongoing struggle within me. At that time, I was in my village home for the Pongal holidays in January, 1973. Each day I would ask God to calm my mind and to give me a sense of peace and assurance about my destiny that I would indeed go to heaven. I received no answer whatsoever.

When I reached the third day I was desperate. I could feel that I had gone partly blind and deaf because of these three days of continuous fasting without food and even water. I was very frightened and my heart began to beat faster. I began to keep saying nothing other than 'I want to go to heaven'. If I could recollect the time well, it was around 12 noon. Since I could not hold myself up I was lying down on the floor. I began to whisper, gathering all my energy and said to God, if I die now, it is for the right cause. I want to go to heaven. I did not know anything better to say then. I was lying helplessly with my eyes closed.

Within moments, I experienced a change in myself. Deep in my spirit I felt convicted of my sins. I began to weep again. I saw something that looked like a blackboard appearing before my eyes, and I began to see all my sins, wrongs, mistakes, errors I have done knowingly and unknowingly, both small and big right from my younger age. But now at the very sight of the reality of my sins, put up before me, I began to weep bitterly and ask earnestly for forgiveness. I was terrified and desperate for help. I began to say sorry for the first time in my life, I admitted that all of these were my sins and asked Jesus to wash them away. Mysteriously, the writings began to get wiped out and more of my sins continued to appear and I felt sorry for all my sins. I began to confess one by one and graciously the blood of Jesus washed them all away. I felt so relieved and at that point that I began to feel the fresh touch of God in my life. I knew beyond any doubt that I was finally free from the burden of all my sins. It was the forgiveness of Jesus that gave me that freedom at last. The assurance of my destiny finally dawned on me. 'Therefore if any man be in Christ, he is a new creature: old things are passed away; behold all things are become new'. (2 Corinthians 5:17). From that day on Jesus became the Lord of life.

As I began my new life in Christ I faced quite a few challenges. My parents began to watch me and my lifestyle. In fact my Amma was intrigued by my new approach to life; and she asked me questions; and then she herself committed her life to Jesus and received the born again experience. As others started noticing my changed life I too started seeing the world around me differently. I found the Scripture more comforting. Reading and meditating on the word of God gave me an unquenchable hunger and thirst for more. The Lord graciously began to reveal his truths and hidden mysteries to me. I could see myself clearly as if I am seeing myself in a mirror. I was absolutely fascinated with my new life in Christ. I needed the power to live a victorious life in Christ keeping away from tests and temptations. The Lord began to fill me with unprecedented joy. I could easily relate myself to the picture in the dream of my childhood. Now I am no more troubled with my identity in my Christ Jesus. My grief and the sense of being lost went for good. I could now stand and fight every time the enemy opposed me with discouragement of any kind.

At this point my father was very much displeased with my new life in Christ. He used to warn me to be moderate with my life. He may have thought I would end up being in full time ministry someday, which he would never agree to and so he even began to threaten me saying that if I continued this way, I would have to bear the consequences. One day he called me aside and said he would even disown me. I truly understand what he meant by saying so, but I was not afraid of him in this important matter of my life.

I began to see the depth and the beauty of God's word day by day. The Holy Spirit was inspiring my heart and mind to be steady in His living word. While I was reading the Bible, Acts of the Apostles chapter 1 and verse 8 stood out before me: 'But you will receive power when the Holy Spirit comes on you; and you will be my witnesses in Jerusalem, and in all Judea and Samaria, and to the ends of the earth'. According to this word, I was graciously empowered by the power of the Holy Spirit day by day which enabled me to be an effective witness. I was given a born-again believer's baptism in a local evangelical church by immersion in water in a pond after I gave my testimony of being born again. I used to attend this small village gathering near my village without my father's knowledge.

When my father came to know of my being a part of this new church, leaving our traditional CSI Church, he became all the more unhappy and furious. The villagers were initially very much hesitant to be associated with me in that church because of my father. He was an influential person in the village, hence they did not wish to hurt his feelings. Since I did not have much freedom to pray and to read the Bible at home, I used to go to this mud floored thatched roofed church in the next village to have my quiet time with my Lord. My joy in the Lord began to grow within my spirit each day.

CHAPTER TEN

DAYS BACK AT HOME

I spent the following two years at home with my parents after completing my B.Sc degree in Scott Christian College. While at home and looking for job opportunities or opportunities to further my studies, I could also invest my time in studying the Scripture and also wait upon God for my future.

It was rather difficult to find a suitable job without proper credentials. As for my father's plan for me to pursue a master's degree, I kept getting rejections from all the institutions I sent in my applications. I could not succeed in getting admission even from a B.Ed college towards becoming a trained teacher. While I was waiting, the time went by and two academic years had already gone by.

It so happened that while waiting, I began to take active part in all the household chores and even to do some extra work. During the daytime, when my parents were at work and my siblings in their school and colleges, I used to be occupied with house work like cleaning and cooking with practically no electric or gas stove available those days. I had to make food with in firewood stoves, which involves much effort and time in scrubbing and cleaning pots and pans covered with thick soot.

At this time, my father suddenly decided to relieve the servants who were looking after our farm animals. We had two cows and their calves. Washing and feeding them and milking them were added to my daily chores. I also had to feed the chickens and the turkeys in the backyard. Feeding our dogs Rover and Jimmy, and cleaning their kennel, too was part of my household work.

Amid my packed schedule, I decided to spend time reading more scripture. Reading the Old Testament was quite challenging. Yet I persevered and reached the Book of 1 and 2 Samuel, named after the person God used to establish kingship in Israel. In the process Samuel anointed both Saul and David.

Saul was the first king in Jerusalem and, later, David was anointed king. David was known both as a great warrior and as the sweet singer of Israel, the source of poems and songs and some of which are collected in the book of Psalms.

The Bible calls David a man after God's own heart not once but twice. The first time was by Samuel who anointed him as a King Saul's successor, The Lord sought for Himself a man after His own heart (1 Sam. 13:14). David was a strong but unassuming shepherd who became God's choice to replace Saul as the king of Israel. He was humble yet self-possessed, readily dismissing human wisdom. His absolute trust in God becomes evident early in his youth, when he kills the Philistine giant Goliath with a sling.

God who is compassionate and pardons those who forsake their wicked ways and return to Him (Isaiah 55:6-7), readily pardons David, when he prays earnestly with a contrite heart, seeking forgiveness and to create in him a clean heart, which is so beautifully narrated in Psalms 51:1-17.

I was very much taken up by the life of David which highlighted the level of adoration and Godly character of David from his young age, his victory over the enemies of the Israelites, and so on. As ignorant and desperate as I was then, I dared to pray to my Lord that I would be more than glad to have my future husband be named 'David'.

CHAPTER ELEVEN

ABIDING IN GOD'S GUIDANCE

While waiting on the Lord regarding my higher education, the spirit of the Lord impressed upon my heart to find out what I have in my hand. I then said to myself that I have these Sports Certificates of merit as I had been a champion in my school and university days. As I have mentioned earlier, I had represented both my school and college for competitions in sports and games like netball, tennikoit and track field events. These memories of my medals and shields that I had won for my school and university came to my mind. I started reminiscing about the long hours of practice on the field and tracks. The Lord impressed upon my heart to send in my application to the YMCA College of Physical Education, Madras University. Envisioning this course of study to be the source of securing a good job, I wrote a letter to this college and in a week's time the prospectus and details of this college with a booklet was mailed to my house address.

I patiently read the instructions. The pictures of the college really captured my attention. The details intrigued me, especially the one about the physical test I needed to take. It also stated that the interview dates will be scheduled in a week's time. I understood that in order to secure a seat in this college I had to undergo different tests to pass the interview that would be conducted on campus. The field tests would include events such as running to check my speed and endurance as well as skills for other field events.

I thought that I was not ready physically. At this point my muscle memory was fading and I saw this as a barrier to pass the tests. I realised that I needed to secure a good score to be selected for this Physical Education Course. I was very excited as I was about to travel alone to

Chennai (formerly Madras), which is about 750 km away from my village. I had never travelled alone to such a far away place, but now I was willing to go for it at any cost. I found out that the only train available was departing at 4:30PM, the next day from Tirunelveli, the neighbouring district which is 90 km away from my home. My father agreed to let me go and my mother helped me organize my trip to Chennai. I, along with my cousin Freeda, who was a teacher in a school in Chennai and was returning to work after her summer vacation. Both of us travelled the next morning by bus to Tirunelveli, in order to catch the evening train from Tirunelveli to Chennai.

Thus, the journey of my life started taking a different direction. Eventually I fared well in the interview though it was very exhausting. I accompanied my cousin Freeda to Chennai and stayed with her in her hostel for a week till the physical tests and interview were over. The interview was spread over 3 days and tested all the candidates for speed, endurance, stamina and skills in their respective sport. The week went by as I ploughed through in anticipation and physical exhaustion from the 100mts and the 1500mts, with aches in my muscles as I awaited the interview on the final day. I not only got selected but also secured the 8th rank among the 150 students who got selected. Praise God!

COLLEGE DAYS IN CHENNAI

My college days in YMCA College were very different as we started the day at 5:30 in the morning with a regular sportswear with strenuous running for 800 meters, jogging followed with conditioning exercises till 8 AM, after which we had breakfast and then attended theory classes up to lunch hour. In the beginning I could not cope with the schedule being too rigid but I pressed on to do my best. The evening session was our specialization, games. I specialized in basketball. Students in this group were coached for different skills of this game and took part in matches within the college groups. I eventually was introduced to various sports and games. During the course we learnt the rules of athletics and games. We were given training to conduct sports events in any given institution.

I came to learn more discipline and order for a better living in and through this college. The highlight of my experience was that we had student representations from different states of India. I had opportunities and privileges to share my faith and grow in the Lord. Even though we hailed from different cultures, languages, food styles etc. we learnt from each other, accepted each other and found harmony in diversity. India being a vast country, it is quite interesting to note that we are so different in many ways and even in skin colour and features but we share the same pain and joy at heart.

CHAPTER THIRTEEN

My First Job

Extremely excited but again the job needs hours of standing out doors for the PE classes and since no indoor facilities were available and the Chennai heat is much to handle, but I enjoyed being able to secure a teaching position as per my father's desire for me.

Two long years went by and I came to the end of my Master's degree course. It was such a joy to know that I proudly reached the graduation day with great fulfillment. In 1979, I graduated the Masters in Physical Education program with honors. The same year I was placed as Physical Director in the department of Physical Education in Valliammal Junior college in Chennai.

When I got my first job in Chennai, I had to look for a place to stay within my monthly salary of INR400, which was a relatively good pay in those days. I was staying with one of my aunts until I could find a suitable rental accommodation. Every weekend and after school hours I walked and searched for places, either in a paying guest home, or a working women's hostel accommodation run by the government or privately owned.

After searching for nearly three months, I could find only a private place which charged three times my salary with an additional deposit amount! So I met the Warden of the Guild of Service Hostel in Chennai, Egmore and gave my application for accommodation. She said there were no vacancies at that moment but would inform me when there was one. Meanwhile I stayed in my aunt's house for a few more months.

CHAPTER FOURTEEN

HOSTEL LIFE AS A WORKING WOMAN IN CHENNAI

Finally, after nearly 6 months, I could secure a place in this hostel, which took care of my food as well. I understood that the warden being a Brahmin enforced a strictly vegetarian diet. However, the warden and other members of staff were very good people. They kept the breakfast and lunch ready by 7 AM, so even for those of us who had to pack it and take it to the workplaces it was convenient. We had a visitor room, which had a black and white TV set with a cable only for viewing news.

In this hostel there were about 90 residents, all from different professions such as school teachers, advocates, nurses, college lecturers, there was even an air hostess, all from different states of India with different languages. I made a couple of friends, three of them who loved the Lord. We looked out for each other daily as we wanted to grow strong in Christian faith by praying and fellowshipping and also sharing our personal concerns and concerns of our families back home. As singing and praying was not allowed in the hostel rooms we used to gather in the open terrace and thus began to grow stronger in our faith.

There was an air hostess who shared the room with me and another girl. She was a very pretty, smart and a very pleasant person to converse with. Her work kept her on a very tight schedule that varied through night and day while I had a regular schedule. One day, as I was getting ready for work, she spoke to me briefly and she invited me to go to the movies over the weekend. Without thinking, I agreed to go with her. To my understanding

I thought it was just going to be the two of us. But as the day approached, I felt very uncomfortable and was confused about this weekend appointment with her. There was a lack of peace in my spirit and I was in a dilemma as to whether to cancel my going with her to this movie or not. Finally I made up my mind and told her that I decided not to join her that evening.

Hearing me, she was so furious that she said something very wrong to me. I did not like it, so when the noon time set in I was very disappointed with how the matter ended. Later I came to know that her boyfriend, along with his friends, came that afternoon in their posh cars to take her to the movie. Sure, I would not have enjoyed her company with those strange boys. Since then, she never spoke to me, rather she was very cold towards me. This marked an end to our friendship. I was very saddened by the events of that afternoon. Thankfully, as I was replaying the events in my mind, someone knocked on my room door. It was the knock on my good friend from the next room as she came to invite me to join the all night prayer in the Moore Market complex in Egmore Railway station which was close to our hostel. Gladly I joined her for this meeting where I enjoyed the worship and intercession for the whole city of Chennai and the country India.

CHAPTER FIFTEEN

CHENNAI CITY

Having come to Chennai and adapting to the city life, I came to have a firsthand knowledge of the attitude, the behaviour and the lifestyles of people living there. To my amazement, it was much different and very advanced, unlike life in a village. But as I was keen on learning to adjust with and understand people who have come there from many states and languages and cultures, I discovered that there was one common topic of discussion, which was common to all of them including my college classmates and colleagues. Their common topic of discussion was movies and the heroes and the heroines, the latest film releases and so on. Surprisingly I did not have anything to contribute to that kind of conversation because from my childhood and up until later years I never went to the movies nor experienced watching a movie in a movie theatre.

I was thanking my Lord that He kept me away from such snares of life. I prayed that I may not be trapped into such practices of life in my youthful days as it could be hard later on to come out from such habits.

CHAPTER SIXTEEN

Back To My Hometown Again

During this period of my life in Chennai, I was working as a Physical Directress in Chennai. Following which I was also privileged to work in Bain School, Kilpauk. One particular day, when I was busy with my students in school, the Principal sent word for me to go to the office to meet a postman who handed me a telegram from my father saying 'Start immediately.'

My father wanted me to relocate back to my village and join a Christian school named 'Ringeltaube Higher Secondary School' in Mylaudy, a town closer to home. I was indeed very disappointed on hearing this, but I had no way of changing this agenda of my father. I believe that my father wanted me to work and stay closer to him and not a day's journey from my family home.

I took the Kanyakumari express train that evening by 6:30 PM and reached Nagercoil where my father was waiting to take me to attend the interview for the teaching job at the Kanyakumari diocese office. I was successful in the interview and was offered a posting at Mylaudy Ringeltaube Higher Secondary School as a Physical directress.

Since my native village home is nearly 45km from the school, I got a paying guest accommodation in Duthie School boarding once again. for the next one year period. At this point of time it was nearly a decade since I had stayed in this boarding school except that I was an adult with a job in hand, what a different feeling altogether.

CHAPTER SEVENTEEN

CONCERNS FOR MY FUTURE

As days passed by I was wondering why my parents were not taking any interest in my future, to settle me in life. Even my schoolmates and college mates kept asking me 'Haven't you found a boyfriend yet? They may have thought that I was not competent enough. And one of them even said, if I remained this way, by not taking things into my own hands, nothing would happen, and by waiting I would only become old and my hair would turn grey. I had no answer to this bleak prophecy.

As far as my understanding goes, in our family such matters were not discussed in the open. My mother would express her concern to me privately but she remained helpless without my father's involvement in this matter. When I crossed the age of 28, our neighbours, my uncles and my relatives would sympathetically tell my mother to look for a marriage proposal for me. The interesting yet strange part was that everyone was talking among themselves but none would dare ask my father.

Along the line, there were a couple of my classmates who wanted to marry me. However, I had decided not to marry any person whom I have met or seen before, so I began to pray to the Lord to reveal His plan for me or send me His chosen person as my life partner. And thus I waited patiently in prayer and the months passed by.

At this juncture, my sweet mother mentally prepared herself that she would like to do something to advance my future, so she came up with a plan to travel to Kerala, where her parents and her siblings were living, to approach them for help. So she planned to journey by herself, early the next morning, taking the earliest bus to reach there. But instead, the following morning she shared about a dream she had in the night, where an elderly person with a brightly shining robe appeared in her dream, and said to my Amma, not to go for this venture for He himself would do the needful at the right time for her daughter.

CHAPTER EIGHTEEN

ASKING GOD FOR THE IMPOSSIBLE, AND RECEIVING IT

A thought came up strongly: maybe I was supposed to be single all my life, so to go forward, I took time to pray to find out what was the will and plan of God in this path. As a matter of fact I was even serious about joining any such organisation to be useful and be productive with my life.

At this point I decided to pray and ask the Lord for His intervention since I am His child. I told the Lord, if it was His plan for me to remain single, let it be so. I also told the Lord to use me in whatever way He has planned and proposed for me, and that I will surrender to his will. I began to pray with earnest longings and desires. The good Lord has been very merciful to me, being fully aware of the customs and the formalities of my village and in our families, where the typical arranged marriage system was being practiced. This was very prevalent in those days, so I began to seek the Lord for His intervention, his leading and his direction to guide me.

By this time, I had seen my college mates and my friends getting married and settled in life. A few of my friends even spoke ill of me seeing that I was 28 and not yet married. Some of my relatives even blamed my parents for not being diligent enough to seek a partner for me. But the Lord impressed in my heart to seek Him and wait for His time. When I fasted and prayed for a specific time, I had a deep sense of peace within me. I prayed to the Lord with the following conditions in my mind;

1. My husband must be a total stranger whom I had not seen before. Saying this, I thought to myself that it was indeed difficult to go about

ordering God to send me a person whom I have not seen before.

2. I desired that I would like to have a chance to talk to my future husband at least once prior to our wedding. I would just like to make sure that he loves the Lord and that he has a desire for ministry and service to God. In our culture in those days, to meet the future husband prior to the wedding was not acceptable and considered an offense. This was a very difficult thing with the prevalent family traditions to be able to meet the future husband since only the elders in the family do the arrangements.

3. I desired for my future husband to first meet my father to ask him for me in marriage even before meeting me. By tradition, only the elders of our family get to talk and agree on weddings and the details. The couple never get to talk to each other or to the parents.

4. Not to forget the request I made to the Lord nearly seven years ago: If He could allow my future husband's name to be David.

After this specific fasting prayer and request about my future, to be honest, I was rather doubtful even to know for sure at this point whether I am called for our Lord's full time ministry in His vineyard as a single person. Yet I continued on. I was working in a high school about 40 km from home. I was a science teacher for the 9th standard boys. On a particular day, on 10th January in 1983, at about half past ten in the morning I was called to see the Principal in his office. When I went to the Principal's room he told me that someone had come from my native village to see me. It was none other than my village Pastor. When I met the Pastor, he gave me a quick report of the purpose of his visit that morning. A gentleman had come to meet me regarding a marriage proposal. I requested of him to give me a couple of hours, which he did; and then during the lunch hour the Pastor took me to the public bus stop about ten minutes' walk where this young man, bless his heart, was waiting all this time in the scorching summer.

When my eyes met this man for the first time the Holy Spirit began to prod me. It was the positive defining moment and I began to be more receptive to His work, not knowing much. I silenced myself with no words. As this gentleman began to introduce himself as David, my eyes began to open, and then he spoke about his work in the Middle East, Abu Dhabi, his job, and his vacation. He added that he had only three days of vacation left. He told me that he had visited my parents in our home the previous evening with the elders of his family. I gathered my courage, and paused for a moment to look beyond him over the miles and miles of paddy fields and the mountain range behind him. I then took a deep breath and introduced myself and I said to myself now is my time to ask this person the following questions about his faith in Christ and following that, about the desire he had for serving our Lord. Our brief meeting came to an end as the school bell rang for classes to commence after lunch break. I was overwhelmed with joy that my Saviour had planned it all, my prayers were answered at last. We then exchanged mailing addresses – postal addresses those days - and he left for his village about 50 km away. From then on I had much to think and to come to terms with.

I was totally convinced that the events were too real to be true. Even after saying goodbye, my mind began to wonder about the name Abu Dhabi which he mentioned I never heard before and I quietly went to the Geography room to check out and found this place on the Middle East map. I was totally humbled when I recollected the sequences of these events. My heart was throbbing in ecstasy. I mean, I felt how God, my heavenly Father, could do so much for such a puny person like me! I was very limited in my faith then, because of my lack of understanding and knowledge about the greatness and majesty of our God. Foolishly I imagined in my futile mind that these were difficult events for the Lord to bring together. Probably my Lord had a good chuckle, looking down at me. But since the Lord Almighty is more than able, He chose to answer all my requests for such an insignificant me, thus equipping me for the journey ahead.

CHAPTER NINETEEN

HINDRANCES TO OUR UNION

Strangely, my parents disapproved of this proposal as my father did not like me leaving home and settling far away from him in the Middle East where my would-be husband was working. In those days parents were the final authority even in matters like this. So I had to wait for a few more months. By now David started writing to me and we were communicating once a fortnight since overseas phone calls would cost a fortune and also that one had to walk about half an hour to a public telephone booth in order to book a 'trunk call' and wait nearly an hour or so to get the connection.

I could never understand the logic of my parents in delaying this proposal. Fortunately my parents could not find another man for me as the days went by. By this time the believers of the church prayed with me for a change of heart in my parents. I fully trusted in God to work a miracle to get us married. By this time I turned thirty and God finally softened my father's heart; and one fine day after five months of waiting he agreed to this marriage. Praise God!

CHAPTER TWENTY

THE DAY OF MY WEDDING

Finally the time was fast approaching for the great day. I was preparing with much joy and the day of June 14th, 1983 had just dawned. Nothing is so merrily celebrated as the union of a man and a woman. Christian weddings in southern India are known to be a blend of Indian and western cultures. A couple of hours before the wedding service David's sister and cousins carried decorated trays containing the wedding saree, the veil, a Bible, sweets and fruits to the bride's home. The church pastor blessed the trays and handed it over to the bridesmaids.

As the groom and family waited, I got dressed in the wedding saree which is traditional silk, a half white saree along with the veil. After this, the wedding procession started to move to the church. All our families, villagers, guests, and friends were seated at the CSI church for the wedding service. David walked in the aisle in front and my father walked with me in the aisle with our church Pastor. The wedding service commenced and that day my father gave my hand in marriage to David.

It was the most emotional time of my life as David placed a golden chain called thali in Tamil and mangalsutra in northern languages, around my neck in the locket on which was embedded the symbol of the cross. We exchanged the Christian traditional vows. As I shed tears of joy, I could also understand that it meant to me a huge blessing as well as responsibility.

After the wedding ceremony the church organ played the exit wedding march music and thus ended the wedding service and the children showered flower petals on us. The entire congregation followed us for the wedding lunch in our home. After the feast was the very emotional traditional event, when my parents and the villagers sent me off to my husband's home with my packed up belongings, and our uncles and aunts and village elders gave us parting gifts from the very home I have been a part of all these years of my life. Personally, more than being overjoyed, I was rather moved with emotions.

We drove out of the gate of our compound in a decorated white Ambassador car, down onto the road to David's parents' home 35 kilometres away. With heavy rains showering down, we drove and reached the destination by that night, where David's parents had organized a party for the villagers and for the family members and relatives. My beloved husband, David Lucas's father is Joseph David and his mother, Palammal David. My husband has two older brothers and an older sister. He also has a younger brother. David hails from a village called Anayadi.

CHAPTER TWENTY-ONE

STARTING OUR LIFE'S JOURNEY TOGETHER

After we got married, there was an unusual delay in obtaining my residential visa from the U.A.E Government, owing to some recent changes in visa regulations. I finally joined David in Abu Dhabi after a couple of years in 1985. Soon after reaching there, I started my teaching career in the Abu Dhabi Indian School.

Even though we share similar experiences when it comes to our family, we had many different views to deal with such as values, priorities of life, wearing jewellery, and so on. Looking back, it was rather a very challenging time indeed. We have been wading through seasons of struggles and difficulties. But the Lord made us stronger in our faith life each day.

I was beginning to know my husband David as a person and it was a new experience in this new place, Abu Dhabi. This was a real life experience. God was merciful, kind and patient with me. David loves the Lord and he has experienced our Lord in a very interesting way. The Lord has been leading David through special ways of hardship to draw him to His fold. His encounter with the Lord is an amazing story.

His initial experience with the early church in the Gulf, especially in Dubai, was inspiring. He was instrumental in the forming of the early Tamil speaking Church in those areas under the palm trees in late 1970s. He was a fine man of God, so passionate that he has to share with the people the love of God he has experienced in his life. He was working with one of the leading oil companies in the Gulf and he was really enjoying working with his Arab colleagues.

David has been benevolent at heart, very skilful and hard working. Very creative in making our children's cribs, beds and custom made study tables for our young growing kids. Once he even fashioned a violin for our children. He has been very skilled in carving and wood work. He always encouraged me to be who I am. Selflessly he mentored our three children in an exclusive Godly way. The reason for our children being whoever they are today is David.

When the divine call came to quit Abu Dhabi, he did not hesitate to come forward to practically follow God with all of us, as the man of the family. Such a daring man of God he still is. He withstood all the odds of our personal life, family life and faith life. He has been a great role model for all of us.

CHAPTER TWENTY-TWO

My Father's Accident

My father and my brother Isaac went to Chennai in 1987 regarding my brother's admission in a medical college after his schooling. He was preparing for the entrance exam to get into the medical college to become a doctor. So they both went to the medical college office at Chennai to get some work done. At one point, as they were trying to cross the road my father was hit by a car. He was in a very pathetic state when he was taken to the hospital and was found to have fractured his arms and limbs and was unconscious with a severe head injury as well. Later he was transferred to a hospital in Madurai where he underwent multiple surgeries over a span of two years. Mercifully he survived, but was very anxious, unhappy and could not come to terms with what had happened to him.

CHAPTER TWENTY-THREE

CHALLENGES IN ENTERING MOTHERHOOD

In the meantime, another painful experience of my life was just waiting. I experienced three miscarriages one after the other, which left me with the question whether I would ever be able to bear children at all? Have I done something wrong? I was filled with much grief, sorrow and shame. Initially we found no tangible reason for this repeated hardship.

There was a prevailing superstition where I come from, that such mishaps were curses of ancestors revisiting us. Again we looked to the face of God desperately. Eventually we were told the reason was to do with the Rh factor. Those were broken times in my motherhood experience; more than four years of painful life.

When I entered my young adulthood, there were thoughts about my future related to motherhood experiences. These thoughts naturally crossed my mind. Growing up as a child in my village I heard many stories about the challenges that came with motherhood, child bearing and things like these. Particularly, this one thought of normal delivery kept bugging me and disturbed my peace all the more when I was in my late twenties. Thankfully, I had made a prayer to the Lord, and then left it to Him to take care of me when the time comes. I also prayed for healthy babies for me. God is gracious.

CHAPTER TWENTY-FOUR

BIRTH OF OUR CHILDREN

After the challenges of the miscarriages, the Lord heard our cry. When I was pregnant, I was very careful with the way I walked and the food I ate and different things I did at this time; I was always watching out. I would not hesitate to say that I was even very sceptical about the 'ordeal' of going through pregnancy. In fact I had to fight my way through to the full term, and when the joyous day came in that Corniche Hospital, Abu Dhabi, both of us rejoiced at the birth of our first child. After nearly four years of waiting and praying, our first daughter Angelina was born. We both rejoiced in God's blessings to our family.

And later, God chose to bless us with our second daughter Adlien and finally our son Joshua. All three of our children were born when we were in Abu Dhabi. The amazing blessing was that I was able to experience normal deliveries all three times. Our children grew up in Abu Dhabi, and went to the same school where I had been teaching since 1985.

CHAPTER TWENTY-FIVE

The Play Of Hormones

Right after Angelina was born, I started experiencing sudden mood swings for nearly a period of six months, starting soon after my first delivery. This included sudden bouts of over-excitement and sadness, irritability and anxieties. Later on I came to know that this syndrome is known to the medical field as 'postpartum depression', which is caused by dips in hormonal levels after delivery. The enabling grace saw me through this, too although I did struggle with this syndrome and initially, I used to dread these abnormal symptoms. Thankfully, for the next two pregnancies I was mentally prepared to face this challenging phase. Thanks to the knowledge and experiences I personally gained in managing this postpartum depression, caused by a devastating imbalance in hormones after deliveries, I was able to help some friends of mine who were undergoing similar experiences in their life.

CHAPTER TWENTY-SIX

Wrestling With Unwanted Fears

When our daughters were born, we decided to travel to India to visit our parents. When we went to my parents' home with our children, the villagers, too, came to see them. Sadly, though, none of them, not even my father, was excited to see my precious daughters. Maybe my father thought the same way as the rest of the people in my village did, regarding the arrival of a girl child to be a financial liability. I am grateful to God that David's parents adored them and cared for our girls.

When Angelina was nine years, Adlien was nearly eight and Joshua was just turning four, a silent fear arose in my mind. Memories of my sister Jiji passing away fifteen years ago when she was barely twelve years of age kept coming to mind vividly as if it happened very recently.

I recollect slowly walking into my older daughter's room in the middle of the night, quietly kneeling beside her bed, laying my hand on her head and crying out to my Lord Jesus to take away the fear of losing her, which gripped me. Then I received the assurance that with my God by my side I can overcome any fear. The fear was gone.

The Lord led my daughter Angelina to become a strong teenager. It is the hand of God which enabled me in my late 30s to have three babies through normal delivery as an answer to my early years of desperate prayers. We were glad to see our three children growing like any other children. They could do their daily chores, school work and other stuff without much dependence and help.

CHAPTER TWENTY-SEVEN

PARENTING IN OUR OWN STYLE

As parents, we never gave room for much screen time to our kids in their regular schedule and we did not advocate or encourage animated TV shows. As a result a lot of time has revolved around us and the family. We regularly practiced family prayers before dinner time, gathered on the couch and sang and worshiped our Lord, read a scripture passage, and we shared our days' events and one of us parents prayed, after which we came together at the dinner table. As our kids were a little older growing up, apart from the family prayer, it became a family practice to gather on weekends or extensively on birthdays and on holidays where we sat around our coffee table in the front room, on the couch or at times comfortably in our bedroom or in one of our kids rooms.

We would continue to write down the points of gratitude or just counting our blessing time and also the pressing problems which mean personal challenges. At the end we took turns to read aloud to the family and we prayed among ourselves for each other. As time went by, one of us would facilitate and keep the time and stop at a certain point and would begin to read our points aloud, even the pressing problems and pray for each other. On birthdays we took turns to affirm the person and make a special event for that day. This tradition went on in our family and is still prevalent to this day. Eventually, this practice has given each of us a good experience and even our growing children have developed this habit in journaling as well, which I think is a good practice.

Even in later years, I think they have not forgotten this practice and wish and hope they still continue to do so even now. These days, there are many kinds of journals in the form of hard as well as soft copy, even online, which

I think is much easier and handy. Looking back, this practice paved a way for a good time investment in our children from our early years.

Another tradition is that after the family prayers, our kids touch our feet invoking our blessings. This normally happens, even otherwise, when they went for an exam or an important journey to a distant country or for an interview or for any such important events. After our parting prayers they bend over to touch our feet, and we as parents touch their foreheads and bless them to go their way, to prosper and do well.

In case you are wondering what this underlying meaning to this act of touching parents/elders feet, the belief is nothing other than as elders who obviously walked on this earth longer than them and as young people, as oldies, they have gathered a lot of wisdom and experience, so by this act they seek the elders blessings which will have a covering over them and these elders will continue to be accountable for them in praying and interceding even while they are on their way.

CHAPTER TWENTY-EIGHT

OUR PLANS FOR CANADA TAKE A DIFFERENT TURN

During this period of our work in Abu Dhabi, we had managed to buy a plot of land close to Nagercoil. It is a lonely place at the foot of a hill away from the hustle and bustle of the city and towns. David and I envisioned that one day in our later years this venue could be a retirement location for us.

However, by then we set our mind on emigrating to Canada in order to offer better education for our children there. So we decided to sell this property. We then advertised this property for sale and found an interested buyer from Abu Dhabi who hailed from a nearby village.

CHAPTER TWENTY-NINE

MY SUMMER VACATION IN INDIA

Meanwhile, our school's summer vacation commenced on 1st July and my colleagues at Abu Dhabi Indian School were making plans for the annual vacation and started booking tickets to travel home. I began to think of my past 18 years of life away from home, away from my maiden lifestyle, and I began to miss home and my family. I realized that spending a vacation with my parents would be an ideal thing to do.

I was driving to school that morning, with Angelina, who had just turned fourteen years that March, in the front seat, and our other two children in the back seat of our car. While driving, I shared with her my desire to visit my hometown this vacation. She said, 'Why not mummy, I will put my hand on yours, while you are driving, and we shall pray that this summer you will get some time to be with your parents.' She did pray and we both agreed on this one thing. That evening she mentioned this to her dad but he said nothing about this then. However, he came back after a couple of days and said that there is just one ticket available in Gulf Air and that I could go to my hometown. I left for India by myself while my husband looked after our children during the time I was with my parents.

Absolutely unexpected, I had a wonderful time beyond my wildest dreams with my beloved parents, most importantly without any interruptions around, just the three of us in the same old family home where I grew up. I thought to myself it's indeed the greatest holiday ever. I would not trade this beautiful experience and the memory for anything.

My parents treated me like royalty. We enjoyed our meal times together and my mother cooked my favourite food. She wouldn't allow me to do anything. In fact, she hand-washed my clothes since washing machines weren't available, but thank God there was an abundance of water supply those days unlike earlier years. Once again, I felt the love of my mother, after being away from home after my marriage for almost 18 years. Amazingly, even my father was so much a changed person. He waited on me, enquired all about my life, our kids who were by then 14, 13 and 9 years of age.

The very special thing I would like to reminisce about was the stories of our parents and especially Papa's special past memories, they both opened up spontaneously and shared freely from their hearts. Both were in their late sixties and seventies and I realized that their hearts and minds are full of memories and unsaid thoughts. I'm glad that both of them poured out their stored-up thoughts and memories. I was really enjoying them even though late nights were very unusual for my Papa who is an early night and early morning person. I had no clue what was lying ahead of me, especially that this would be the last time ever that I would spend time with them, especially with my Amma. She told me about her days in Munnar, her growing up days there and her married life and how they had a lovely time together. Amma added the stories about my Grandma Annie Isaac, her mother-in-law.

This time my Papa interrupted and began to interact with me and came up with his story and shared his life in Aramco, Saudi Arabia, and about his father and mother, how they brought them up and about his five older siblings. By now I was sitting at the edge of my chair. I was in fact blessed to hear from him about his humble beginnings and the sacrifice of their parents to feed them and the discipline and training he received from His dad who was an evangelist, the beautiful stories of how my Amma came in his life all the way from Munnar. Thankfully he could acknowledge openly now and also shared about my Amma being so hard working and loved by all and began to stutter and weep about my mother's hearing impairment and how her inner ear was badly affected that even surgery could not help.

Papa narrated the details of his accident. In spite of the multiple surgeries he had to undergo, there was irreparable damage to his leg, resulting in a limp in his walk. Most importantly, he acknowledged his love for my mother and his appreciation of her for being with him in the hospital after the accident; invariably being there every day waiting on him patiently, expressing her love for him and being sacrificial. He began to narrate all the details related to that time of his life which was so sudden, hospitalized for many months and he still continued on to talk about Amma's sacrifices for him.

Papa enquired about my younger sister Suji and her family who were in Abu Dhabi at that time. He was also very happy and content with my youngest sister who was newly married and moved to Gurgaon, New Delhi. My father was proud of my brother who worked hard in his studies and skills to become a well-known orthopaedic surgeon.

Once again, he reverted back to his olden days of his busy life, in serving the people in that village and getting into Government services and few of his personal challenges with the higher authorities. I was filled with tears when he carried on further with our childhood and he was silent just mentioning the name Jiji and paused for a moment. Once again, Papa began to stutter about the death of my sister Jiji; and he could not explain much about her. So I thought he was regretting not being able to love her the way he should have as he never expected her to pass away so soon, being barely 12 years of age. He regretted that he himself, being a medical person, couldn't save her. Both my parents were very tired and weak but they had each other for company.

In my futile mind, the big picture I had built that my Papa being such a hard person, was not easy to relate to and the barrier I experienced with his anger and other tough nature began to crumble and I started to see him like any other struggling human, trying to find a balance to live and accommodate himself to this life. As humans, at some point in life's situations, we need to come to terms with it and be reconciled with our past. I was so happy that these times were so profound and meaningful. I regretted having wasted many precious moments in the past and early years of my life, having to think of those times when I was longing and yearning to receive tender love and being hugged, being embraced with love and to sit on my father's lap.

Those are a few of my feelings which I could not bring up now. I would call those feelings and unmet expectations as having a 'street kid attitude' which was a heavy burden on my back. But now, coming to grips with the magnanimity of willingness and to voluntarily forgive and receive forgiveness released me from the entanglements of such traps but the fact of the realization is that my Papa was only a human, a physical person.

Those days were experiences of God's forgiveness in our lives in the form of God's signature in our family especially to my aching and longing heart.

It was a good reunion, building a new level of relationship and I think it was a kind of winding up and closure. There was love and intimacy shared so freely between us unlike any other times in my life. I never realized that there was no more time left for us. Indeed, the old stories really added richness to the heritage of my life. Pain and hurt clouded my mother's mind, but the beauty I saw in her was that she was even willing to move forward. Anyways the good and the bad events make up our life's journey. There is so much to trust in Him the only One God who can exchange them for our good.

CHAPTER THIRTY

THE TAPESTRY OF MY LIFE

Looking back at my life, I must say it was beautiful. Each event, each interaction, thoughts, decisions, every bit of love is like a thread in the tapestry of my life. It seems without rhyme or reason day after day, dark threads are woven together often but, in the end, they form a beautiful picture. The dark threads are the difficulties and disappointments, the trials and tears, and these are also necessary because they make the bright threads look all the brighter and help give your tapestry its richness and glow. No one has ever woven a tapestry quite like our God and no one could have, as 'my life is unique' I realize later. All the good things - the happiness and fulfillment, the love we gave and received, the lives that we interacted with and influenced are the bright threads. Not knowing what was ahead, I had returned to Abu Dhabi and joined my beloved family.

To add on these precious memories, times were not the same again when I saw them after three months as things had drastically changed. It was like the sweetest ever times I had, like a small window of time I could always cherish.

Sadly, Papa was experiencing dementia, Alzheimer's and he could not recognize me after that. My mother lost her hearing ability so it was a very saddening experience for me altogether.

CHAPTER THIRTY-ONE

God's Calling To Serve In India

In the year 1998, as we were living a comfortable and pleasant life, we were planning our emigration process to Canada, It so happened during these months that the sermons were from the book of Acts of the Apostles, which is in the New Testament. The grand truth about the amazing acts of the apostles, their venture and boldness urged the early Christians to be challenged to go about their calling. These lovely messages ignited our hearts and minds to carry the Gospel to the lost souls.

As a family, we along with our children started praying about reaching the lost souls. Having heard the gospel, we thought it is best not only to be served but to serve without any delay. At this point of time after listening to these messages, many events directed us to decide that one thing that is needful as a family is, 'reaching the lost souls.' Reminding ourselves of the history of the early disciples of Jesus, details about one of the disciples of Jesus named Thomas who even doubted Jesus, had come to India and laid down his life as a martyr not far from our home village - a twelve hours journey by train - which till date stands as a memorial as 'St Thomas Mount in Chennai'. By now I was gripped with an unusual urge in my heart to serve the lost community and bring the light of God's salvation to the people in our homeland. We shared this desire with our children and engaged them in our family prayers to prepare them for this big change, at some time in our life.

Not only the powerful scriptures, the living testimony of the servants of our Lord Jesus and even the words of a song written in 1979 by Dan Schutte published in 1981 –The words of the song are based on Isaiah 6:8.

The Lord of Land of sea and sky
I Have heard my people cry
All who dwell in dark and sin
My hand will save ...
Here I am Lord. Is it I Lord?
I have heard you calling in the night
I will go Lord.... –

This song stirred my heart for several days, weeks and months to adhere to the call and the will of God, not to mention the vivid encounter which was growing very strong and more powerful and was compelling my spirit to obey even in the night watches as the world around was quiet.

These experiences were thrilling, yet coming to the place and to the spot where he was leading was the reality and a mysterious part of it. Even today, after many years now as I recollect and begin to live in those moments in my memory tracks, down the lanes, it is not easy at all but very scary. Now I realize why some of our good friends and family members tried to discourage us and tried to stop us when we decided to come on missions, as the feelings they had for us was not to suffer the consequences in taking such bold steps.

Personally whenever I encounter such experiences, I begin to process whether what I allow myself to believe and my thinking is going to be practical or not as the events ahead were unknown and unfamiliar. The scary part was, once we stepped out from the stable life we got engaged in then, we could never reverse it as we would be like burning the boat and all the bridges behind. It was indeed like icy cold water running through my veins, an absolute terror and hopelessness. But with the eyes of faith all things looked possible.

The thing that held me in faith were a few lines of the songs I the Lord of sea and sky- by Daniel L. Schutte, the stirring refrain of the song and the different words of the song like 'whom shall I send, here I am Lord, I have heard you calling in the night, kept me pondering even more deeply. The following lines, I will go Lord If you lead me, I will hold your people in my heart. Resonating with the lines of this song is the scripture Isaiah 6:8 made me begin to think of those precious yet unfortunate village kids especially in the village of Erachakulam in southern India.

They became my heart's desire and gradually became a possibility if not now but maybe at some later days or years I thought to myself. I am sure the Lord has been working behind the scenes, always directing me to the course of action. As in the quote by Francis Thompson in Hound of Heaven, 'I fled Him down the nights and down the days'. In every human life, God is already in a loving pursuit to do His will through each person's given lifetime. So, I was filled with mixed feelings. To be honest, recollecting even now this journey was only made possible with our amazing God and His surplus grace though it was quite scary. Only a big God like our Lord Jesus could back us up and drive away all the fears and doubts to move us forward step by step all these years.

CHAPTER THIRTY-TWO

A Divine Call We Could Not Resist

Everything works together for good. In 2001 I came and visited my parents and those were my memorable times. Spending elaborate times around the table, talking and listening to stories of their past life. After a week, I went all by myself to our property in Erachakulam to clear the land and to do the needful to sell it. I stood in our property in Erachakulam considering the sales and documentation waiting for the interested buyer from Abu Dhabi who promised to come and meet me on 7th July 2001, who also came down for her vacation to India from Abu Dhabi, unfortunately or rather fortunately she never turned up.

That bright morning, soon after I entered the land, standing just a few meters past the gate, God spoke and conveyed His desire for us, as Lucas' family, to come on a mission, to help the village and the kids here with a school. I was not sure about anything that was happening that bright morning. At that very moment I knew I heard Him, and His call was very clear. wasn't audible but deeper than a voice, an impression I could not erase or get over it.

God sets apart His people for His service when our hearts are yielded and surrendered to Him. He then uses us to do his work. God is the one who gives us the desire and he is the one who fulfils that desire. All along, both David and I had a deep desire to serve our loving Lord and Saviour. God prepared our hearts and minds through hearing the word of God in our church in Abu Dhabi. Our hearts were really concerned for the needy people in India, so we decided not to sit back and be served, but to go out and serve. So we surrendered our lives for God's work. The love for Jesus and His clarion call which says 'The harvest is plenty but the labourers are few' made our hearts throb during the silence of the dark nights and to obey His loving and tender voice, to serve Him in His vineyard.

There was a strong convicting voice deep down in my soul and spirit. And I decided never to stand against it but to only obey and follow wherever he leads us. There has been a chance to hide it within me but this divine call became so strong and true that I could only submit and surrender even though there was a huge uncertainty about the future. There was opposition and obstacles, hindrances on all sides but there was peace and serenity only in the presence of God. Without much delay I returned to Abu Dhabi.

Before I returned from my native place to Abu Dhabi, I shared with my mother the heart of God for our future, that we should start a school for the downtrodden in India. During my stay with my parents during my vacation, l had developed and cherished a new bond now, more than the past years, a loving friendly relationship with my mother. She was the first ever person there with whom I could share the call of God for our family.

The following were the last words she could say; most significantly she said, 'You go to Abu Dhabi and I will pray for you and the school you are planning to start here'. I was sure and knew that she prayed for the fulfillment of God's will in my life. She was listening carefully to me and assured me of the success of future ventures ahead of me and my family. Since she was a teacher by profession she indeed had quite a few tips to share with me, which was precious. Sadly I never realized that those were the last audible moments of her life. Later that year she went to be with the Lord.

It is sometimes difficult to understand and obey God's will as it requires faith and patience. It is natural to want to know all of God's will at once but that's not how God usually works. He reveals to us one step at a time, each move with a step of faith, and He expects us to continue to trust Him. The important thing is that as we wait for further direction, we are busy doing the good that we know to do. As the scripture says in James 4:17a 'If anyone then knows the good they ought to do and doesn't do it, it is sin for them'.

God says in 1st Samuel 15:22, 'Obedience is better than sacrifice and to heed is better than the fat of rams.' Accordingly, I preponed my trip and returned to my family back in Abu Dhabi. When I reached home, I was initially hesitant to explain my experiences to them about the encounter I had with my Lord. I sat down with my family and explained the prodding in my spirit about the call to serve in this village. When I expressed my thoughts, my husband and my children began to understand the divine power behind that call. The first thing we did as a family was that we decided to seek God's counsel in prayer for a period of time and waited for His approval. We as a family started to fast and pray during this period, and at the end of it, we also shared this matter with our church in Abu Dhabi. The church earnestly prayed over us.

We were answered with peace in our hearts; so we unanimously decided to go to India within a short period of three months. We even got the courage in Christ, to give up our secure jobs with lucrative pay in Abu Dhabi. I was filled with a mixed feeling of joy and pain within me but I strongly knew in my spirit that if God speaks, He is also sure of how to execute His plan. All I needed to do was to adhere to His call.

Even though we had to face some obstacles in getting release from our jobs, God made it possible. Initially the employers were not willing to let go. However, after a couple of meetings with us they favourably considered our request and accepted our resignation letters on September 11, 2001.

When we shared this with our friends and our family in India, they felt that we were out of our minds. During the 1980s and 1990s, the chance to go abroad for work, especially in the Gulf was considered a great thing. Getting a good and secure job in the Gulf was a common aspiration among many Indians those days. Therefore many advised us not to leave the Gulf.

We never dreamt of resigning from our secular jobs as we were very comfortable with it. But when we got the call from God to be in His vineyard, we could not refuse. We gave up all possessions and positions we had in the Gulf and followed Him. Thinking back on those events now, it was an option for us like something that Moses had experienced. He considered it good to to suffer with his people rather than be called the son of Pharaoh. He refused to be known as the son of Pharaoh's daughter. He chose to be mistreated along with the people of God. (Hebrews 11:24-25).

CHAPTER THIRTY-THREE

ADDRESSING VARIOUS CONCERNS

The overwhelming sense of uncertainty about the different facets of our life at times overtook our resolve to serve the Lord; and tried to block us from the journey we were about to embark on. Desperately sensing the enormity of the task ahead for our mission work in India, we decided to be specific about our heavy concerns, needs and desires even before preparing to move to India, rather than being vague about them. So we started to list them all one by one as they came and clouded our minds. After making this list, we started to pray over these specific points in this list.

All of us took time even to continue to place the list before our Lord and this helped us to lighten our mental stress and load. Coming to think of this method, it was a very helpful tool and also a good exercise as we even now have these prayer points with us as a road map; and continue to pray over some of them. Looking back over our shoulders the past 20 long years we can boldly say that God has been a faithful Father all along. There is no doubt about this. He had never failed us.

Specific prayers bring specific answers. Lord Jesus, even before healing the born blind, Barthemaeus who was crying out to Jesus for mercy, asked him what he wanted Him to do for him. Jesus was looking for a specific answer from him. The blind man was specific, too, and said, Rabi , I want to see. Jesus then said, 'Go, your faith has healed you'. (Mark 10:49-52). Here is the long prayer list that we made before we embarked on our journey:

1. To be effective in the education ministry through our experience, skills, knowledge and qualifications.

2. To educate the people of the village in Erachakulam village in the love and the knowledge of Christ.

3. To start kindergarten classes for 50 students and provide them transport facilities to reach the school.

4. To get dedicated, committed, God fearing, experienced teachers and other staff with the capacity to love children and work with us sincerely.

5. Honest office assistants, engineers, builders and auditors.

6. Support and cooperation of the village leaders, political leaders, the general public and the community.

7. To make Jesus a reality in our school project as we work among the local people in the village so that they might catch a clear view of our vision from the beginning of this project and support us.

8. A good church fellowship, constant favour and support from church leaders and fellow believers to stand with us long term for this commitment and supporting prayer partners who would be accountable for the very purpose we are here.

9. Be good stewards of the precious opportunities given to us.

10. For admission for our Children, Angel, Adlien and Joshua in a Christian School with loving teachers, good friends and also be able to cope with the immediate culture and environments.

11. Our children to have a vision for their personal lives and start imparting it in the long run and embody Christ's love and values in their lifestyle.

12. To raise a two-bedroom house in the existing facility.

13. Never to lean on human strength, influence, threat, power and principalities that might deviate us from the calling and vision the Lord has laid in our hearts.

14. Temporary discomforts, inconveniences should not discourage us but strengthen us, make us bold, confident and to trust God completely.

15. To be a role model for our children and the school family we are going to raise and to practice what we preach.

16. To have a far-sighted vision with definite goals in mind to go ahead with plans for 1 year, 5 years, 10 years, 20 to 50 years.

17. Not to compete with other institutions around the area, which might discourage us with negativism but to draw new insights, knowledge, help and support from them if needed.

18. To be good stewards of the finances we receive from our jobs and funds.

19. Continue to depend on God's supply of wisdom and to be cautious about the reminder that the heart is deceitful above all things (in Jeremiah

17:9).

20. The evil and dark forces in and around the campus, idol worship in the neighbouring blocks and the crematoriums in the proximity will be nullified by the precious Blood of Jesus and these properties be donated or converted for God's Kingdom's work.

21. To discern people with ulterior motives, with the power of the Holy spirit and the scripture and be able to judge instantaneously.

22. Never to neglect our quiet times with our Lord to be guided and strengthened by His voice and in His word since it's easy to be carried away by the intricateness and the multifaceted details that need our time, attention, thinking, planning and working.

23. Perfect and vital and an ongoing relationship through the day with the Lord.

24. Genuine love to be shared among us as a family, which will generate the inner strength, so together to oppose and resist and to withstand the enemy.

25. Both of us, David and I, are rooted and grounded in the word of God to guard ourselves with the full armour of God on an everyday basis.

26. To be deeply committed to each other and willing to be corrected by each other, if necessary.

27. As we are aware of the dowry system prevailing in this part of India, and as we are not setting apart any savings for our precious daughters for dowry, the Lord will prepare committed life partners for our daughters who will take their hand in marriage.

As we lay at the feet of Jesus, we surrendered all that we had and ourselves, so that the Lord could use us for the extension of his Kingdom. By the divine will, call and plan of God we both resigned our jobs and on September 11 2001 and were officially relieved from our responsibilities. We then packed our belongings and started our journey to our homeland, at this time most importantly laying aside our long cherished dreams to settle in Canada for good, knowing fully well that our Lord has His own ways of directing the water course in the direction He desires. He is sovereign, so He has our life's reins in His divine hands.

CHAPTER THIRTY-FOUR

SAD NEWS ON THE EVE OF OUR FINAL MOVE

Life's big decisions require big changes. As we were at the final stage of packing to leave Abu Dhabi with our tickets booked with Gulf Air, at around 2 AM we received a phone call saying that my mother was found to have cancer in her ear and was given a very brief time to live. This shocking news gripped us with grief and we travelled all the way with the pain of the sad news. My brother was waiting to receive us all when we landed at Thiruvananthapuram Airport. It took ages to clear the customs formalities before we could head home to see my mother. We stopped for an hour to see my mother on our way to our rented house in Nagercoil, about 45km away from my family home, with a truck load of our belongings.

Even in her pain my mother hugged us all and had a warm smile on her face. Sitting beside my Amma's bed was my father crying inconsolably with bitter tears. I stood there helplessly and crying as well. Unexpected events unfolded right in front of me! The warfare with the enemy started even before we could begin our work. I thought to myself if the enemy could be so furious, how much more zealously the Lord would protect us and pick us up from this muddy water of uncertainty and hopelessness! The experience with my mother was too painful even for our children.

I was totally broken as she was the only one person who stood alongside me apart from my beloved husband, all through life's journey. Though there weren't mobile phones and WhatsApp messaging those days, my mother and I used to be in close touch through snail mail fortnightly for many years. Now all expectations of hopes of being together with her ended that moment. It was a tough battle in my mind. I was not yet prepared mentally to accept something like this. In fact, while packing up to come to

India, I was imagining and having silent conversations with her in my mind; imagining that she would be pleasantly surprised when I give her the gifts that I brought along with me. I was excitedly looking forward to enjoying her company again, and was happily thinking of those beautiful moments I was about to share with her. But all those sweet moments were snuffed out in a moment of time. I could not ever have imagined that she would never hear me again because her inner ear was very badly affected by cancer.

It is a mystery that when we are in the hands of the Master, we neither understand some of the events, nor the future of our own lives. We are as clay yielded in the hand of the Potter. He is in a continuous process of breaking, melting, moulding and filling us; so who am I to question the Maker?

On October 31, 2001, as we drove toward our rental house in Nagercoil, the daylight had faded and night was setting in. We carried our aching hearts and minds up the stairs to the first floor of this new place, as a traveller in the middle of a desert. We slept that night with all our suitcases and boxes around us as if we were in an airport waiting for a transit flight.

This rental house was to be our home in India for the next eight months, during which period we got busy with our school construction work on our property, and advertising for staff and students.

CHAPTER THIRTY-FIVE

A NEW ERA BEGINS

Morning dawned and we got our children ready for the new school, which was just a kilometre from our home. This day, the 1st of November 2001, marked the beginning of their life away from the known and the familiar Abu Dhabi. David and I took them to their new school and went through all the formalities to enroll them there. For our children, coming to India was always a happy holiday trip to visit grandparents, be away from school routine and so on. This time when they actually walked into the classrooms in their new school, the difference with the system of education was really hard to adjust to, especially for our son Joshua as it was not the holiday season of chasing squirrels, catching butterflies or playing with chickens, lambs and the neighbouring kids. On the contrary he had to face a new school system at this school here in Nagercoil, which took him by surprise and he could not get adjusted to it for a long time.

This was the first challenge for all of us. One day he refused to go to school as he developed chronic stomach pain and could not concentrate on his regular classes. The first year at school, we as parents went through a tough time with our children having to go through this kind of experience. Gradually, they were able to adapt and make necessary adjustments and continued their schooling.

CHAPTER THIRTY-SIX

GOD WORKS IN THE HEARTS OF OUR CHILDREN

According to the scriptures (Isaiah 54:13) 'Your children will be taught of the Lord, and great will be their peace'. God enables even young hearts to obey and follow Him, and by this our children would come to know that it is God who has given this promise to us.

Amazing is God's perfect way, much more than we could comprehend. The plot in Erachakulam village, where we started our school project, was a long forgotten desolate area, situated 5 km away from Nagercoil city. This place was filled with adultery, idolatry, poverty, alcoholism and there was even a crematorium near this plot. The village children here are sadly involved in child labour. However, praise God that there have been amazing changes here over the years. There are many Christians now worshiping the one and only true God, and many lives have been transformed today.

Interestingly it's God's plan that he had set the stage for His plan to unfold even before we could think of this transition. While we were still in the Middle East, we had purchased this property through a friend of ours for a holiday rest house. This property is under the foot of a hill, just a plain and empty land with no electricity and no running water. Now we have made this property our home and school complex. We raised a proper concrete School building.

We lived in this property and worked with this community. It's so rewarding now to hear such joyous singing and praises and even scripture verses from the lips of these precious children. Not to mention His marvellous and divine protection and courage to withstand the threats and opposition from religious fundamentalists who questioned our work. There were also interrogations from officials who gave us difficult and challenging times over the years in this village of Erachakulam. We raised the school to be a government approved primary school. As more students were enrolled in the school, we started our first session of classes in June 2002.

David had been blessed with a mastermind for the work we are called in here. By nature, he has been strong-willed, very courageous, decisive and creative; and a very hands on person. He had been a great builder, a prayer warrior and even used to counsel the villagers untiringly and involved them in any possible productive useful way as appropriate. In the school, David used to take scripture classes and moral classes too. I would say David has also been very much efficient in carrying out official works related to the government and public related assignments. He has been a strong pillar and a stalwart for the mission works for years. He was a vibrant preacher and had even started the first ever Tamil Christian congregation under palm trees when we were in the Middle East.

We as a family witnessed the hand of God guarding and protecting us from the stronghold and warfare of the enemy from time to time. Gradually, we were comforted by God's soothing presence, which was the healing balm to our grieving hearts. On the other hand, over the years, we literally battled against wild creatures like python, cobras, vipers and other wild creatures, yet no harm had come upon any of us all along and we praised God for that. Each step we took we have been encouraged by our Lord to become very strong under the canopy of His hand.

In the first year of our coming to this place, according to the heart's desire and prayer of our children, especially of Adlien, the Lord blessed them with an opportunity to visit our friends in Abu Dhabi for about two weeks. Our friends were happy about our teenage children's passion and excitement about the work in this village. A few of our friends visited our place and even stayed with us along with some of our school students.

I took care of the school administration from the beginning, which included planning, organizing, directing, supervising, inspecting and evaluating, also setting up goals, review, feedback and innovations. It was the sheer mercy of God that has endowed me with such amazing grace, wisdom and understanding all along. Amidst many testing times and challenges, I have personally encountered God's unfailing hand of support. I used to be a very sensitive person, basically a melancholic but over the years the Holy Spirit has transformed my temperaments and is even now moulding me for His purpose so far. My favourite verse is, 'Not by might nor by power, but by His spirit, says the Lord'. (Zechariah 4:6).

Not to forget the reality that the sudden shift and change in the living conditions, school systems, not having friends around and the living style here had really affected our children very much. As parents, it was hard to see them suffer as they came along in gradual transition in life. However, they started adjusting to the new environment and even, in their free times, availed opportunities to visit the homes of our school children in this village.

CHAPTER THIRTY-SEVEN

VISITING AMMA IN HER PAINFUL TIMES

I wanted so much to visit my mother and stay with her these days but with the newly started school and with our children in this new set up, it was quite challenging. So, David used to fill my position at school and thereby enabled me to visit my mother once every month. Now, both my parents were in my brother's place, with medical care and treatments in his hospital. So sad to see my Amma in intense pain. She was still fighting this illness.

The thing that amazed me was that she was still trying to speak to me in that hospital bed in a very feeble voice. She shared her wonderful dreams about her home above, which she so beautifully portrayed to me, and that was so comforting! During one of my visits to her, she said about a dream she had about a postcard with just three points written on it and she added saying, 'I might need to settle these three sins and be forgiven.' I used to be so helpless to convey to her what I would like to share from my heart but, considering her total deafness caused by her disease, I tried to bring her comfort by making hand gestures and lip movements. Thankfully she seemed to understand and in this way I was able to communicate my thoughts to her.

Her smile and her attitude with which she responded was worth remembering. Sadly, she was in unbearable pain, losing weight, losing appetite and the last time I visited her she said to me, 'My home is ready, I see the bright lights!'; and she was pointing to the corner of the ceiling above her bed and asked me also to look at this beautiful place she was looking at. I too nodded my head and kept smiling at her and gestured to her agreeing to the joy she was trying to share even at this stage of her life.

As true believers, the pains of this mortal body are not compared to the future glory ahead. I too partook of her hope and her future beyond here and now. I only wished to spend more time with her at this time of her life. She needed someone who understood her and was around her. I was glad that I was there to listen to her story and be with her on her journey as it related to us all as humans. I am sure there were multitudes of angels around her at this desperate state of her life. What a way to experience and witness the grand departure and the entry to the home above, which is prepared for each one of us far beyond this world with all the pains and disappointments.

There is never a sunset without a sunrise, a glorious and splendid sunrise; that is the promise of God to us. Whenever sunset comes our way, we need to remember that God will certainly bring a sunrise too. Whenever there is a low moment, a shadow that falls across our paths, when disappointment darkens the way and the last glimmer of hope fades from sight, when the chill of the night closes around me, we need to remember that the sunrise awaits us with all its life and light and glory and brilliance. And just as our God has promised, the sun will rise the next morning, the sunrise of God's love will light our life again.

No matter what sunsets you may encounter, I know my God will always bring us through every night to a better day. The time was up that day and I needed to return to my family and check on my children. At the end she continued to advise me to look after our children and she prayed for our family and our future and our endeavours. She held both my hands and kissed me and I bent over and kissed her forehead for the last time.

Receiving her prayers and blessings, I left her, motioning to her that I would visit her soon. But the same week, the day after Christmas, 2002, Amma reached her destination when she left this earthly abode for her future home. As a family we grieved over the loss of my mother who was the only comfort to me as her daughter. I was deeply overcome by the power of love which I received from her all my life. The flames of love that ignited my heart over the years now was snuffed out as she stopped breathing, I was left watching her lifeless body as flashes of memories flooded my mind. But I chose not to grieve over her any more but to celebrate the King of kings for this rare gift given in my life and to others in the family as a representation of His love on earth - God El Shaddai.

CHAPTER THIRTY-EIGHT

WARFARE AND STRONGHOLDS

'No weapon formed against you shall prosper' and God will be the fence around his people.

Initially this property where we started our school project, was a barren land, the area was full of uneven rocks, filled with human bones and rubble. It was a desolate wasteland and the nearest homes were the colony of villagers which was at least a kilometre away. There was only a pond, a mountain range on one side and three crematoriums on either side. No doubt the locals warned my husband not to venture outside after 4PM. We came to know the history of the property. It was apparently a hide out for robbers and murderers, a place where liquor was made illegally; a place of adultery and all things detested by our God. Not a safe place to stay; no running water, electricity, nor street lights. Darkness prevailed all around not only literally, but spiritually too.

Such was the scenario. It was not a logical move, but the children and the people in here were our target. Unless someone ventures into this place as God's people, these communities would be forgotten. We stood firm in faith as we faced warfare with evil forces during these years. The hand of God was with us like the pillar of cloud and pillar of fire all around us during the day and also at night. Because of this, we never felt alone and stranded which was amazing as I recollect; and also we celebrate.

The ongoing guidance, support and assurance by the unfailing power of the Holy Spirit was beyond understanding as we started everything from scratch, which cost us our precious time, energy and effort. God has anointed my husband with an ability to foresee and do most of the planning and manual jobs, along with other workers. David continued to work on a daily basis for many years now. He used to start in the morning and work till late in the evening. He used to work with his hands and so his hands and fingers were calloused yellowish and pale in colour and felt lumpy and rough to touch. He never regretted being a part of His mission here.

Logically anyone viewing us with the world's eyes could see the hardship and disapprove of our coming to India. The reason being, as we had worked overseas, they expected us to come to India and live in a decent house with all the luxuries. When they saw us among the local villagers they were surprised. But over the years things have changed. This place has now become like a well-watered garden although it was once a parched land. It is now a Christian school; and because of this school we have easy access to the community and are able to fellowship with them.

In the year 2006, we received sad news that my father had passed away. We were again grief-stricken and I was reminded of how short life is.

CHAPTER THIRTY-NINE

HOPING IN GOD TO MOVE FORWARD

Where God led us, we simply followed. The faithful Lord has kept us all safe till this day. Obstacles and heartaches were a part of us but the serenity in our hearts and minds is unexplainable. I recall one of the slogans we used to say among the five of us: 'We are holding the fortress'. A few times, when we had financial challenges, strangely enough our children used to speak words of encouragement and comfort us. I used to wonder if they even understood the magnitude of that financial crisis. Even when they were young, we used to regularly have our family devotions both in the mornings as well as in the evenings. Listening to their humble and honest prayers has broken my hearts to bits. The faith they declared each time made me even ashamed of myself. Bless their hearts. We never lacked any essentials nor did God forget us. Our Lord has been our shepherd. As this place is close to the mountains, on several occasions we had to put up with wild creatures, but God who has given us all the authority in heaven and on earth has kept us safe.

A few times we had experienced wild creatures on our campus, terrifying moments like when a venomous cobra raised its hood hardly a metre away from David. In those moments God sent his divine angels to protect and save him and kept him from any harm. During the early years, a python had eaten our pet rabbits. Another time our chickens were stolen from our farm. For a few years the village drinking water supply was refused to us.

No evil can come near us as our future is in His hands and He is holding us in the palm of His hands.

CHAPTER FORTY

ANGELS ALL AROUND US

One evening both David and I were called at 4 PM by some government officials for an interrogation meeting. They were very harsh and rude and one of them kept on asking both of us many questions related to our coming here, our job, our intentions, our family etc. Our son was all alone at home when we got back home very late, nearly around 2 AM with heavy hearts. Right then, our land line began to ring and some voice from the other end began reading Psalm 91 in a soothing, comforting voice.

I had never heard such a voice before. This was to remind us of His comforting presence. I listened to this voice till the last verse; and the verses still ring in my ears till date. I told my husband, who was standing beside me that someone was reading Psalm 91 at the other end. It was just a soothing balm to both of our souls. I wonder till today who this person could be, I'm sure it was an angel of the Lord!!! 'A thousand may fall at your side, ten thousand at your right hand, but it will not come near you'.

CHAPTER FORTY-ONE

THE VILLAGE WITCH DOCTOR

One evening after a tiring day, an elderly man was knocking on our gate. We took him in and we found out later that he was the witch doctor of this village. We came to know that he had already openly challenged us in the village, our family and our school saying that we would be driven out of this place and that we will not be able to withstand the power that was with him. That evening in his conversation with David he kept wondering how we stayed on at this place with our young children, a lonesome place without a neighbourhood and he openly expressed his surprise and was very inquisitive about our safe stay in the school campus, even at nights.

David told him that if he would like to get the answer to his question he should come and see inside this campus after nightfall. He became even more curious. It was then that David explained how our Lord himself comes down with a fiery wall of protection around us accompanied with angels and fiery chariots and that is why we are safe and do not fear anyone or anything. For anyone that walks in to harm us will never be able to lay a finger on us because of this divine protection. He nodded his head without saying anything and immediately took off saying goodbye.

CHAPTER FORTY-TWO

A Mother's Brokenness, Waiting For A Healing Miracle

For 26 long years I had been earnestly waiting in prayer, crying, and fasting for the healing of our youngest daughter Adlien who had been suffering from a skin allergy since the 50th day of her birth. We tried many ways for her healing. She underwent numerous tests suggested by doctors specialised in the field of dermatology, but it seems to us that the good Lord had kept the healing away from her for a time for a purpose.

As a child she could not eat properly, nor sleep well; and because of sleepless nights she could not fare well in her studies and score good marks. Yet she loved the Lord and prayed every day, earnestly longing and waiting for deliverance. She needed to keep away from many of her favourite food items that would aggravate her condition. Whenever she tasted any of these, she had to go through painful consequences. But her love for God as well as her family kept her going. We were all growing in God each day as we kept separating our lives to please God and keep us more sanctified. As our child was in great pain, we could only go to 'The greatest Physician' after having gone here and there for medical and prayer help. We trusted our Lord more and more each day.

These past 26 years have taught us more patience, trust, humility, and obedience. Who are we to question God? We are engraved in the palm of his hand. Nothing and no one can take us out of his hand. Soon one day I shall know the reason why God allowed these many years of pain in Adlien's body. While all the other children of her age enjoyed everything as normal children regarding food, sleep, good grades at school and ability to wear any outfit, Adlien was restricted to cotton fabrics etc. As a family we surrendered and submitted to the will and plan of God more and more each day.

CHAPTER FORTY-THREE

David Survives A Major Health Issue

In 2008, in the month of January, David was invited to minister at a place about 700 km from our home. He was away from home for about 10 days. This village is again a Hindu locality, he had to travel through many small villages without proper transportation and not many other basic facilities. He did his best in preaching the good news, praying over the sick, counselling etc. Many were saved, baptized and came to faith in our Lord.

While returning on the 1st of February in the train at about 8 AM, David began to feel a pain in his chest. He thought to himself it might just be gas and never thought anything beyond that. When he reached home at about ten in the morning, he felt tired but never suspected anything serious. As the pain began to increase, later that evening he said he needed to see a doctor. We rushed him to the nearby Catherine Booth Tucker Hospital where David's ECG was recorded. The doctors froze and refused to tell me anything but, they instead immediately wheeled him to the Intensive Care Unit.

I could only see puzzled faces around me. Later by 11 PM the doctor told me that he had a massive heart attack and we needed to make sure by waiting for further test results. This hospital was not equipped to treat heart patients. However, praise God, the first aid and care which was given there saved his life. I started to look to Jesus for help and comfort. Our girls were in their colleges in Chennai and Joshua was at home preparing for his exam, so at this juncture instead of being sorrowful and desperate I clung to Jesus and waited on Him for help and strength as it was already midnight sitting by myself at the hospital corridor

Away from home, I just can't express how lonely and helpless I was at this point. I was unable to communicate to our children about what happened. My situation was very pathetic, just holding on to the promises of God. Gradually by gathering my inner strength, I finally informed both our daughters and son and they reached the hospital very soon. Praise God David was declared out of danger after 48 long hours of waiting. Our good and merciful God has lovingly taken care of David and he could come home within 10 days. The wonderful, wounded hand of our God preserved the life of my husband. Even today he is a living testimony to the healing power of the Lord for this village and the students of our school. Many of our friends, family and church family prayed and God answered us. Glory be to His name.

CHAPTER FORTY-FOUR

THE PRAYER POINTS OF OUR DAUGHTERS

As our daughters finished with their studies and got into jobs, they also came to a point of contemplating on their future life and family. Both our daughters were in their mid and early twenties. They knew from the early years we have been praying for their life partners, asking the Lord for God-fearing men for them both.

At this time of their lives, they began to list the details of the man each of them desired and brought it to our regular prayer time. Knowing fully well that God doesn't answer vague prayers, they took their journals and listed the traits describing the man that God was giving them to marry and we also made it our specific prayer for them. Even as our girls were praying specifically for a particular person, they visualized him and became strong in their faith and knew that God would provide them with the right partner.

When the right time came, God answered their prayers, that they had prayed for and what they visualized came into a reality. Amazingly true stories of their lives - praise be to His name.

CHAPTER FORTY-FIVE

ANGELINA BREAKING TRADITION WITH HER LIFESTYLE

The dowry system is very much prevalent in the culture of Tamil Nadu from ages ago. Parents usually begin saving up for the future of their girls even from the early years. In our case it was a different order, probably it happened so as God wanted to show us that His riches are sufficient for the future of our daughters. We could not think of saving gold and cash for their dowry. Instead, we invested in his Kingdom.

Having said all this in my life, a time came when we were in the process of leaving the Gulf for good and it struck me so hard that it nearly became a paramount concern. My colleagues and friends made it look so obvious that without saving money for dowry we could very well anticipate a rough time in future. Some of our friends made it look like we were bad parents heading for a bigger disaster without enough savings in the form of gold and money for our daughters.

This had been a burden bugging me all along with my other concerns, which I wrote down and all five of us agreed and signed it and left it for the care of our Lord. The prayer looked something like this 'Lord, as we have not saved any cash or gold for our daughters to give them in marriage as dowry, you have to see to this request and fulfill our need.' This point, too, was added to the other concerns we prayed for during the same week we were leaving for India.

Angelina worked hard in her school studies and she finished her final exams with good grades. Unlike many other young girls who aspired to join in a financially secure field of studies like medicine and engineering, Angelina chose to join YWAM (Youth With A Mission) in Beach Centre in Chennai soon after her schooling. She underwent Discipleship Training School (DTS) and Ministry and Leadership Development Studies (MLDS) while there and served in YWAM for two more years.

Later, she passed Bachelors in Business Management (MBA) through Distance Education in Madras University. She then obtained a student scholarship loan from an Indian Government Bank and went to Singapore and did another MBA from Raffles university U.K. university. Later, she studied MA Psychology through correspondence in Indira Gandhi National Open University in Delhi.

While in Singapore she got a job at Khoo Teck Puat Hospital, worked there for two years and paid back her student loan. And in the year 2014 a fine gentleman, Koshy Mathew took her hand in marriage without demanding any dowry. Angelina got married on 28 July 2014. She, too, had no deep passion for gold and ornaments. She chose to model an exemplary lifestyle for the community to be the ideal bride in the society with bare minimum gold on her wedding day.

It was easy for Angelina to break culture and social practice since she was already living in God's culture. It was surely an answer to our prayers made exactly 13 years ago. Our Lord provides. He is our Jehovah Jireh. Angelina made a choice again to move from Singapore to India and is happily married and is now blessed with three children.

CHAPTER FORTY-SIX

ADLIEN'S DREAM TO GO TO EUROPE

Our second daughter Adlien was very interested in art. She had been drawing, painting and recording videos. She has a collection of her artwork. She is a good singer too. Growing up, she desired, but could not get into any music school for voice training because of the skin allergy and the medication which kept her from regular sleep hours; but she was a hard worker. After having finished her schooling in Nagercoil she, too, joined YWAM in Chennai Beach Centre like her sister. Later she enrolled in Women's Christian College Chennai to pursue Visual Communication.

With the ongoing skin allergy the climatic conditions in Erachakulam was not conducive to her. Even as she desired and was praying for healing, she was also looking ahead for her future options for her studies. She longed to go to Europe for her Masters. She applied for and obtained a collateral loan to go and do her Masters in Media and Communication in Brunel University, London. She could not find a job there, and so she came back to India and waited for the next door to open. Meanwhile she worked in Mount Sinai and taught Arts and craft. After two years of working with us in Mount Sinai school she took a teaching job in an arts college in Chennai.

It so happened that while she was in this arts college in Chennai, she was invited to participate in an international Conference in Chennai. There she gave a display of her art work on stage in a live program. Guests from different nations were invited online. Both our son Joshua and Adlien attended the conference which continued for four days.

Many other works were also displayed along with the art works of Adlien. One of the guests from overseas, a lady, was really touched by the message portrayed in that piece of artwork by Adlien and bought and took it along with her to her hometown in Switzerland where she shared that painting with her friends circle when a young gentleman by the name of Toby tried to contact Adlien on seeing her work.

Miraculously, over the next five months, he invited her over to Switzerland and introduced her to his family and Church friends. He visited us in our village along with his parents and his Church Pastor and got to know about our work in India and about Mount Sinai School. In a year's time he proposed to her and they got married on November 12, 2016 in Switzerland.

She is still very active in art work online and very creative too. She is blessed with a son Caleb David who is now four years old, and a daughter Amaeya Zadie who is one year old now. Adlien and her family are presently living in Switzerland. The best part of her life is that the allergy that was a stinging pain tormenting her for years is now totally gone from her body. God knows His perfect time for everything.

You can follow her art work on Instagram @apaintedpoetry.

I am sure you will be blessed by her work.

CHAPTER FORTY-SEVEN

CLOSING DOWN THE MINISTRY AT MOUNT SINAI SCHOOL

After her wedding, our older daughter Angelina joined the International Justice Mission as a Psychologist. However, in the year 2018 they both prayed and waited for further direction for their life. They were led by the hand of God to come to Mount Sinai School to give us a hand and support us in the school ministry. They willingly left everything behind and came to stay in the school campus along with their three children under six years of age.

Most unexpectedly, the Lord God had a different plan for the school ministry. The Coronavirus pandemic started setting in a year after Angelina and husband moved in. This pandemic, which caused global havoc, resulted in drastic changes in the education system throughout the country; and our school was not an exception. We had to close down physical classes but classes could be continued virtually. However, it generated hardly any income, not even to pay the school teachers.

Almost two decades of our toil in this village, at the School, have gone by. The pandemic topped the many roadblocks we faced in running the school. We waited at the feet of the Lord for days not knowing how long this situation would continue. Most students of this village could not afford online classes; and the teachers also started leaving one by one. We needed to make a decision soon. All through this, God gave us supernatural rest and peace about everything happening around us.

As a direct answer to our prayers, the Tamil Nadu Government made a wonderful decision to step in and help the underprivileged students of private schools like ours. The government decided to absorb these students in their own English Medium schools. Amazingly, the government is now providing free education as well as free books and other benefits, which enable the students to plug in and continue their studies. This turn of events gave us a sigh of relief because students of government schools also enjoy additional privileges such as special quota for professional courses. Angelina is presently working as a Clinical Psychologist and Facilitator of Plumm Health Ltd.

What comes to our minds is that we were privileged to lay a strong foundation for the lives of these precious children whom the Lord entrusted in our hands. It is now time for us to move on.

CHAPTER FORTY-EIGHT

FALL AND FRACTURE

On a Sunday evening of August 2020, David and I were sitting and relaxing on the outdoor bench to catch the evening sun setting behind the hills of Erachakulam behind our compound wall. After a while I got up from the bench and while making my way around the backyard to come to the front my left foot slipped over a six inch slope and fell down and fractured my left foot. I was taken to a private hospital and treated but somehow the pain got to a level which I couldn't handle both day and night.

So my husband took me to my brother Isaac's orthopaedic Hospital in Marthandam where my brother did a surgery on me and I ended up in a second cast. For days now I am very limited in my movements, thereby I am confined to crutches, walkers and to a wheelchair. I have been through weekly, monthly reviews and gradually but steadily improving as I am writing part of this book during the eighth month of the surgery.

I am experiencing more ease now, slowly but steadily. I am thankful to the Creator for the wonder in fashioning this body. Off and on I go online to check the intensity of the fracture in my case. I was blown away by the intricateness and the wonder of how diverse my ligaments, tendons and bones are formed by the Creator in order to enhance all movements. The wonder of it all and even more the healing mechanism and the process that go with that even though it takes a definite period of time.

I was very much limited in my movements and activities. Instead of having to question and be unhappy I chose to be grateful and take time out to recollect my past years and decades of God's faithfulness. Indeed I have plenty of time to recollect them one by one, causing me to plunge into the wealth of memories hidden of years gone by. I consider this a rare opportunity to be surrounded by God's love and forgiveness.

WHAT IS LOVE?

Love is caring. Love is reaching out. Love is holding back words when not appropriate. Love is taking a moment on a busy day to give someone a word of encouragement. Love is Jesus. He is always there for us. Jesus wants to be our closest friend and confidant and He will always be there to help us grow in knowledge and in God's love.

I cannot even imagine the wonderful things that await me in heaven - best of all, love. The love I will experience in heaven is the purest and deepest and richest kind. This love is perfect in every way and it will make me feel more loved and more complete than I have ever felt. What a day that will be, rest from my labours, joy from my sorrows, recompense, for all the life experiences and eternal bliss.

CHAPTER FIFTY

BLESSINGS PROMISED TO OUR DESCENDANTS

'As for me, this is my covenant with them,' says the Lord. 'My Spirit, who is on you, will not depart from you, and my words that I have put in your mouth will always be on your lips, on the lips of your children and on the lips of their descendants - from this time on and forever,' says the Lord. (Isaiah - 59:21)

I still remember a friend of ours who came to Erachakulam from Abu Dhabi. She spoke to our daughters separately, to find out about their experience here and to ask about their coming to India, if they would have it any other way at this time of their life. They both gave a similar response that they would prefer to stay here and continue to be with this village, with the school and work with these under privileged children. Actually, they were more at home having come here and living with these people.

As parents, bringing our children in their teens to come and live here was basically a huge culture shock for them as they were in a third culture lifestyle. Their identity was in question and yet they were also able to display their trust in their own God in their life situations. There were struggles which we cannot deny. However, they got through all these, as God has fulfilled their desires and He continues to use them as vessels for the extension of His Kingdom as adults.

CHAPTER FIFTY-ONE

TO MY DEAR FAMILY

These past long years have gone by which were the milestones of God's faithfulness and majesty displayed nearly seven decades now, and I am pleased that I happened to meet you all along the way to live together for a few precious years with joy, knowing you in such an intimate way sharing our lives together. So you are now qualified, and get to read this legacy letter and have a better picture of me, Annie. While I pen these words down, I must admit that I may not have anything big and much to leave behind for you all but I choose to include all of you in my legacy letter.

I. To David, My Beloved Husband

You have been a champion throughout my life. I have learnt much from your life's example. I am amazed by your courage and boldness. In fact you are a fighter in the true sense like the man after Gods own heart. Thank you for putting up with my carnality. You have taught me to be generous and giving. The latter part of the year 1977 you prayed under the shade of the palm tree after your work in Dubai with your knees plunged in those hot Arabian sands, that's when you started the first ever Tamil Church and the congregation in the Middle East. People can forget, times can change but the Lord never forgets but keeps record of all we have done for Him with a sincere heart.

David, your passion for our children is beyond explanation. You have custom-made their cribs, beds, study tables, violin and even when they are grown up you never stopped your creative works.

David, when you were hospitalized after the heart attack, the doctor came to the ICU ward for his morning rounds and found you missing from your bed. To his surprise you already had a shower and walked to your bed with dripping wet hair. The doctor looked at you surprised, and said that you have done the wrong thing by having a bath without assistance. At one point, you were advised to undergo open heart surgery which you never agreed to; or to any kind of surgery for that matter.

During the course of those months our children and I begged you for days also for the bypass surgery, but you were determined not to. Finally after a few days you relented and when you were taken in for the angioplasty procedure, the stent would not get through because of excessive calcification of the vessels, so the procedure could not continue. Once again you refused to have any more procedures.

One of those days in the hospital, while you were in bed sleeping, you had a vision where you experienced a sudden flow of fresh blood going down your chest into your arteries and blood vessels with a steady flow in your heart like a chatter of a continuous flowing of a brook of fresh water, which you explained was an easing effect which you had never experienced before. David, since then you were convinced that you had experienced a divine touch and you felt much comfort thereafter. But whenever you tried to be overwhelmed with work and lacked moderation both physically and even mentally you say that you sensed an occurrence of pain in your chest again.

David you continued your great service with your life in this village. In one of your check-ups we came to know that the wonder of God's creation includes a back-up plan for your heart, which had already set in. This is called a collateral circulation. This supplements the blood support for the heart. Coming to know of it, there is a network of tiny blood vessels which in normal conditions are dormant. When the coronary arteries shrink to the point that the blood flow to the heart cardiac muscles is limited (in the case of coronary artery diseases) the collateral vessels may enlarge and become active, taking the place of the main arteries. David, your heart has now switched over to this collateral supply.

Years later in 2014 when Adlien needed to get her bachelorhood/single status from the Ministry of External Affairs in order to get married to her sweet heart Tobias Marcus in Switzerland it became a slow process and she had to wait for about one year. During this period David you were frequently appearing before officials, being sent from one office to another being shuttled from pillar to post not knowing what to expect during those uncertainties and heartache, which was not very helpful to your heart. We experienced an unusual delay. However, David, with your red file packed with all relevant papers and documents you would dress up and leave home day after day without giving up. Finally one fine day, miraculously we received the stamped certificate. The dream day arrived when Toby and Adlien were happily married. Through it all David you have done well.

There was another event which happened in Joshua's life six months after the event of David's heart attack, when Joshua's results were out from his Higher Secondary School. When Joshua applied for the furtherance of his university studies he was rejected and at that time David had an urge to call the admission officer. When he did call, it so happened he got a disappointing answer from the other end saying that the admissions are over and the classes have started since a fortnight and then I heard David requesting the officer to reconsider if possible.

Till this day I wonder what happened the way it happened, as a week later the same officer called our home landline and said, 'Please send your son immediately there is just one seat available in Aerospace, if only you can make it by tomorrow morning in the Chennai office at 10 AM.' The distance from home is 750 km. As we were puzzled and debating about the journey, he called the second time and said that we have decided to pay for the air ticket for your journey. So David decided to send me with Joshua. So we were able to reach the office on time the next day and carried on with the formalities and a brief interview during which the officer said, 'The day after your father called about the admission for you somehow I kind of lost my sleep and rest and when this opportunity appeared miraculously I was glad as your fathers voice was ringing in my ears so distinctly.'

By divine intervention one seat was miraculously made available especially for Joshua! Today he has successfully finished his Aerospace Engineering and continued to do his masters in the same college and passed with distinction. This was not by our might nor by our power, but truly by the Spirit of God. When we were helpless in this remote village, God himself came to our rescue as our Elder Brother. God is our vindicator.

Something about David's voice, while preaching and even talking, comes with power and authority. God has given David this powerful talent and gift. Even in his previous office in UAE there were incidents when he would converse over the phone during official calls, people on the other side would like to see him in person. His voice is so captivating and powerful indeed.

Coming to David's rare dreams of heaven, it was one of those days in his mid-twenties when he was in Chennai city hunting for a job and failing. He often had to go to bed hungry without food. On one such night, when he prayed and went to sleep he witnessed a ladder that was connected to heaven from his bedside. He saw beautiful angels in a row, holding trays of delicious food items descending from heaven and each one took turns to hold David in their left hand and fed him a morsel of the food they had in their hands. Amazingly when David said I am full now, the dream ended and never again he faced this situation without food in his life.

Another encounter was when David was at his first job with his company in the United Arab Emirates and he was down with chickenpox. He was alone in his room with a burning fever. During this time one night, when he was struggling with unbearable body pain and was trying to sleep, he suddenly experienced the gentle blow of cool breeze sweeping through his aching body. Strange enough he felt the numerous scabs on his body beginning to dry up and the fever left him at that moment. As he got up he saw the scabs all over his bed and on the floor. He could then clean the place,the very next day he resumed his duty.

II. To Our Beloved Grandchildren

I would like to foresee for myself and for all our grandchildren the beautiful future through the minute lens of hope and faith far into the years of your future. Congratulations to all our grandkids. I am glad you all joined me just in time to hear me speaking through these lines. I am very proud of each one of you. I am very sure the words of this book will certainly encourage you and give you the grand picture of your roots in detail, where you all came from. You children may not have a clue how thrilled and excited to see the day when you will read and understand these lines yourself, without anyone's help. I am very privileged to have you as my grandchildren, thrilled to bits when I envision now, even when your own children can read these few lines your Grandmamma has personally written to you beyond time and space. You know what, before you were born we prayed for you and when you were in your mom's belly we prayed for you and even now after seeing you, touching you we still continue to pray for you.

You must know this verse in Psalms 139:16, which says 'Your eyes saw my unformed body,all the days ordained for me were written in your book before one of them came to be.This is about you children and what the scripture says. You know you did not appear just like that; you have strong roots beneath, which is very strong and firm. You are so special. Now it is your time to outshine the darkness and make the light of Jesus shine brighter day by day.

Having this background knowledge and also knowing who you are I am very sure you will certainly unlock many doors before you. Lack of this knowledge of yourselves could keep you bound in darkness, bondage and shackles.

In fact, with this advantage to your benefit of knowing who you are, will offer you the strength, ability and access to the world around you fearlessly. As the hymn writer, Maltbie Davenport Babcock wrote, 'This is my Father's World'. Do you know that, you never had to waste time, to grope in the darkness of finding your true self. Your Father God is the Creator, the owner of the whole world; so you have no excuse not to try to reach for the sky, even if you fail you will fall among the stars.

Again, never ever make the mistake of comparing yourself with others for anything whatever the matter is. I tell you,this is a vicious venomous circle which has no end at all. Just believe in the wealth of wisdom and knowledge the Lord Almighty has deposited in you even before the foundation of the world. So keep on multiplying and soon you will see the increase. Hope to write more to you all personally in the days to come.

III. To Angelina, our first born

Angel, although you are a delicate darling among the children of our family, you are the one who comforted me the day I was very low in my heart about the snakes eating away our rabbits; and you said to me the most revealing and profound words, 'Amma, they are not coming to our territory, we have actually come to their territory.' That day made a change and a shift in my approach over all that was around me. I see a lot of leadership qualities in you. You always did well in your studies. We cannot forget the time you shed bitter tears when your brother and sister never matched up to the scores or grades you expected them to achieve, whether it be a competition in singing or elocution you won prizes.

When you completed your school finals you approached us parents to permit you to do the YWAM DTS in Chennai. I was ignorant of such a course, but you researched and were keen to study and then work under them instead of rushing to medical, engineering technical or teaching courses. You told us, as a tribute to God you want to invest in this course. Eventually you graduated through Distance Education and later went to Singapore to pursue Masters in Clinical Psychology. You even found a prestigious job as part of a fellowship, where you have been testifying of God's love to many.

You also took a very rare decision to resign your dream job to hold hands with Koshy Mathew in marriage. He is the man of your heart and both of you complement each other. I am amazed at the way God kept His word and brought you two together, Praise His name. After nearly three years of marriage you both announced your decision to help us by taking the responsibility of running the school. May God bless the heart of Koshy who felt the burden for the school, the students and the community and in fact he took the baton off our hands and began to run the race for the rest of the years with his strong and able hands. Well done, both of you! God is never a debtor. He will surely pay you back what you have invested for the kingdom's purpose. God has blessed you both, with three precious boys. They are the rare gifts from above.

I cannot wait to see them growing up! Avidan is so gentle, pleasing and bright in studies. Zuriel the second son is strong-willed, daring, very technical, taking the lead; very compassionate and loving to the core. Liam is such a darling and just the baby of your family. To me, recollecting your babyhood, Liam is a carbon copy of you at this time of your babyhood features. It's so true that history repeats itself.

Koshy Mathew, you have joined our family according to our prayer. You, being the beloved son of committed missionary parents in north India, have displayed high standard of life values indeed. On July 28 when you held the hand of Angelina our daughter, and walked with her in your brand new journey of life, you fulfilled the prayers we made earlier in life. Interestingly, you never had any expectations of dowry as in the prevailing cultural traditions of India. Not only that, in about three years, you and your family came to Erachakulam to take over the school with all the responsibilities going with it.

Indeed I admire your lion-hearted boldness! I would say, you have come to serve the community and to give your best with all that you have, and all that you are. Once again you gave it all, not looking for any return. With your mission oriented heart and mind you nearly fulfilled your parent's visions and experiences in this needy village I think. We both have witnessed your sacrifices, creativity, commitment and tenderness to the villagers and the downtrodden kids. Both of you together, made it possible for the regular devotions for staff and students, and offered them fellowship and motivation in times when needed.

I remember the regular coaching sessions you conducted for the boys at school as well as for the village boys which is commendable! With many obstacles and hindrances, both of you stood strong. Nothing could match the impact you and your family left on the hearts and minds of young and old here in this village. Scripture points out in Proverbs 19:17, 'Kindness to the poor is a loan to the Lord and He will repay.' As you move on in life, we will continue to bless you, May the Lord bless you and your family and the generations to follow.

IV. To Adlien, The Darling

You, dear Adlien, have gone through much in your growing up years but have emerged victorious. You are like your Appa who is a fighter. You found hope in the healing power of the shed blood of Jesus. You have been a dreamer all through life. You are strong-willed and very creative. I appreciate the fact that you are very strong in your convictions. I have witnessed many battles you fought even as you were growing up, with friends, in studies etc. But nothing could stop you from the destiny God had planned for you. Your children Caleb and Ameya will surely bring you comfort and joy. I am pretty sure what you both as parents dreamt in your life will be fulfilled in them. Caleb will continue to grow in the wisdom and the knowledge of God. He will grow to be a person with a different spirit as per his name. Caleb will be blessed with a strong will power to be different from many who are compromising and trying to flow along the current mind-set. Caleb is a loving, gentle, sensitive, caring, and intelligent boy. Amy is a baby with a strong voice; might become a vibrant spokesperson for His kingdom. She is very beautiful and content to the core. Let's wait and see as she grows up. Our God is still on the throne and is in the process of making each one of us in His plan and for His purpose.

You went to Greater Noida, Delhi and endured the adverse heat and cold of North India where you taught English to the older people of other nationalities. Later you went to London to do your masters and after which you took up a job as a lecturer in Chennai before you got married and moved over to Switzerland.

Tobias Markus is your man of God's choice and he came all the way from overseas to seek your hand. God's ways are past finding (Isaiah 55:9). As the heavens are high above the earth so are God's ways higher than our ways. It was truly a dream come true when you placed your requests before God.

He took it over as His personal case. Even with many obstacles nothing and no power could thwart His plans. He is the ultimate and He has the final say. Toby is a very special person God has added to our family. He was also involved in the work we did in the village and partnered with us financially for the school, which is remarkable. He visited us from Switzerland; and also took us there for a visit and very passionately cared for us.

V. To Joshua, Our Son

Joshua, you are a fighter yourself. Bold, intelligent, hardworking, you followed your dream to do a Masters in aerospace amidst many obstacles. Your hurdles began from the day we left Abu Dhabi. You are like the Joshua of the Bible who faced opposition and battles. You kept on climbing the steps, entered the university, faced a different challenge with your health, needed to swim upstream but you pulled through valiantly. A few of your fellow students even gave up and discontinued their studies, but you kept on. We are very proud of you Joshua, you are a winner.

There even was an opportunity given to you to step down for a year and to take a break but you continued on which proved your integrity. On the onset of bashing storms against your sails though you bent low you kept your calm. At the end, you scored the best scores and passed with first class. You had no problem to get into the Masters in Aerospace. You had to put in a lot of hard work but you again stood among the top rank holders and passed with distinction. Well done son!

Job opportunities were a challenge in your field of work and you took this opportunity to do your DTS in Basel, YWAM centre in Switzerland. You had a rare chance to do the outreach and conduct open air meetings and to share the Gospel in few middle European countries. After returning, you joined our Mount Sinai School and taught the students Mathematics and extracurricular activities and built their hope and moral values.

You also made plans to emigrate to Canada and started to work with all the documentations IELS and even to the point of Biometrics when you had just finished with all official proceedings and formalities and began to wait for the passport request from the Embassy which was the last requisite to stamp the visa for entry in to the country of Canada. However, the doors to Canada were suddenly slammed shut by the onset of global Coronavirus in the month of March 2020 when all the official proceedings were stopped and any further intervention was an impossibility.

So you continued to look out for outside opportunities because our Mount Sinai School, too, had to be closed because of this pandemic. Your present job is with a software company as a research analyst. I know you can bloom wherever you're planted. Joshua, you certainly have a great future ahead. My heart yearns for you to be blessed and to experience many breakthroughs in life more than you can think of.

Joshua, the way you took care of me when I fell down and broke my ankle and needed help to move out of the spot, even within the very first few minutes of the accident you came up with a few first aid measures to help me ease my pain and drove me to the hospital. At every step, son, you were there for me even when I needed frequent dressing for a wound I developed, you did it, time after time without any hesitation. It would not be wrong to say that I often experienced the gentle touch of the great Physician Jesus himself at those times. May you prosper, son. Your dreams and plans will blossom. It may look to be dry and not much is happening at the moment; but mark my words, great seasons are ahead for you.

Grasia, welcome on board to the Lucas family, Being the latest addition to our dear family, do know that you are the answer to our hearts deepest prayers. Knowing you, according to your name you are gracious too. As I have come to know that you fear God our Lord and you excel academically as well. We see you being a great life partner for our dear son Joshua, May the Lord bless you and keep you. May you be an example for many and be a mother of millions.

VI. More About My Siblings

Even though we are four girls and a boy born to our parents, my sister Jiji left us all much early in her life. About my sister Suji, she had married Robinson, my husband David's younger brother, and was blessed with two children, Beryl and Adam. Sadly Suji left this earthly abode and entered into glory when she was 40 years, leaving her husband, young daughter and son behind. Suji had a very sweet personality and has been very stern in her decisions. Even from very early in life she used to make her point always very clear to us, even to my father for that matter. I can recollect when my father had that terrible accident, she stayed home alone and looked after the paddy fields, workers, the farms and the household work being all alone.

My brother in law was devastated with the passing away of his dear wife, yet the comfort of our loving God was his strength in those grieving moments for him and for all of us. Eventually God sent Chithra into his life and he married her, to love him and to care for the children and to support the family.

Beryl is the older daughter of my sister Suji, a sweetheart of your beloved mom and even though she had a brief, but a quality time with you, since she was a loving mom and she did all she could to bless you with all her packed love during her brief time on this earth. Believe me, I still can recall her lovingly calling you, 'Berry..!' her voice still ringing in my ears. Suji had endless dreams for you. Beryl, you are very pretty and a smart girl. You have been a part of the Sunday School, AWANA, and you have excelled in every field you have been involved in. I am very proud of you, my child. You have been a swimming champion in your school days at Abu Dhabi Indian School.

You have also been a champion in the track and field events and bagged many awards, even securing the most coveted position as National Championship record holder. You have yet much to achieve in life. Now that you are married I wish Subit and you a blessed family life. May you both live long with much love and joy unending. Your younger brother Adam had the privilege to be with you from a very young age.

Adam, I wish you great success and blessings ahead. Daddy loved you so much and Beryl has been a best friend for you, too. With all the hardships of younger days, you grew to be a smart young man. You are a very creative person and as I understand you are pursuing your dream of visual communications.You will do well in life. I know you will be a winner.

Adam, you are a smart and intelligent young man.

Isaac is my only brother named after my paternal grandfather. He is the pride and joy of our father. Our parents called him Suresh. I cherish the memories of growing up together in our family home at Paloor. Unfortunately you, Suresh, did not know about our Grandma and Grandpa as they went to be with the Lord prior to your birth. I recollect the memories when I had the opportunity to help you out with the school work and train you for your school singing competition, scripture memory etc. I know you really enjoyed the company of our beloved sister Suji, as both of you were just a year and a half apart and I recollect both of you playing together, both walking all the way to school together, being in Sunday school together. Sooner in life she had to part company to reach her heavenly home.

When you started to pursue medicine to become a doctor yourself, Papa was very happy and I could see his dream plan for you coming to a fulfilment. In the early 80's, I have personally witnessed your hard and sincere work towards your entrance exam for the MBBS. You have faced much struggle to reach the top in the ladder of life through climbing each high rung. Congratulations you crossed every barrier and have reached the pinnacle I would say. Suresh, you are a role model to your beloved children. You paved the way by moulding the course of their life.

Besides all of this, the difficult hurdle was, when Papa met with the terrible road accident, that too, far away from home. You handled the situation all alone, to get him to the hospital for medical help and also continue to focus on your studies. In spite of the trying situation with Papa's life being in such a challenging and in a critical state, you never deterred from your focus and direction. If I am not mistaken, the incident which birthed your desire and passion to become an orthopaedist was Papa's accident, when you witnessed the complications with Papas bones and muscles which took nearly a year to get back in shape. I think at this point you resolved to work towards specializing in this field.

You have proved and you excelled in this field to invest in working on patients with orthopaedic issues. This branch of medicine that focuses on the care of the musculoskeletal system with more than 200 bones in the human body is amazing!

The crowning responsibility you took upon yourself was, caring for our parents so lovingly and tenderly. Heaven has been watching over you both. Human appreciation will never match up to what you have done for our parents. I have no more words to thank you for your extended hands to our parents in their helpless period of time such as their old age. I assume, when our time comes to part this earthly home, we will certainly come to know what it will be, the desperate need of the hour, of old age then. You did well my brother, you have paid a great down payment, well in advance. Well done! To be very honest I couldn't get over this fact for a long period of time. Time will be the only healer, in certain unexplainable events; so please understand me, my brother.

I would like to add this important recent event which brought us both together was the 'my fractured ankle' situation. You did the surgery on my bones and I have seen that you have done it to your best ability. When I happened to stay at your hospital for about a week, I had first-hand information about your hospital. You have achieved your goal, my brother.

You have saved many young and old from the most tragic state of helplessness back to their normal lifestyle. Keep it up. May you live long to see the best in life; may all your dreams and desires of life come true. May Ashly and Areen fill your life with rivers of joy and blessings.

I am really thankful to Sheeba, your lovely wife. The saying goes like this, behind every successful man is a woman. I am indeed very proud of your devotion to our parents all along your married life. The pains and the trouble you took upon yourself to drive our mother to various medical facilities for check-ups and treatments, juggling your responsibilities with your growing children at home, even with the hospital management and official commitments. At some point you even cared for both of our parents, by keeping them with you.

Sheeba you have a wonderful strong personality, May the good Lord bless you with lifelong health and joy. Sheeba, you are the strong pillar behind every success of your dear family. Your disciplined prayer life and the commitment to your untiring services at the Isaac Hospital are amazing.

Ashlee you have been a joy to all of us with your genuine and gentle welcoming smile and your sweet nature is very captivating indeed to be around. I admire your caring nature. I marvel at your talents in music. You have indeed mastered the art of playing guitar with true zeal and passion.

You make me wonder how you made this dream a possibility.Understanding that playing on your own is much different from performing in a group, you need to have put in a down payment of several hours of practice sessions. I wonder how you managed your music experience with the professional studies in the medical field. Well done, keep it up.

I would like to record here,from my memory lane, during the occasion when I came much closer to you was, when I was recovering after undergoing surgery with the fracture of my ankle. A couple of times you met me and I indeed experienced personally your gentle care over the hurt and pains both physically and emotionally. The Lord has entrusted you with the anointing of an expert physician, I could see that far, Ashlee. May your hands continue to heal and restore many in your professional journey

.

Areen, you are the darling of our family. I would like to point out one thing, as you share your birthday with your loving father you also have stolen his heart of love to yourself. I am truly proud of you Areen, since you have indeed fulfilled my childhood dream to become a doctor myself in order to serve the community of mothers and children. You have already bypassed the initial hurdles and are presently in the medical college and pursuing your medical studies.

I am amazed and thrilled with the display of your singing skills. I only wish and pray that the Almighty God will anoint you more and more in your calling; and through your special skills and talents may you draw many into our God's Kingdom and His unfading glory. At this time of your life, may you shine with supernatural wisdom, courage and confidence, to outshine any prevailing darkness, to be the bright shining star. I wish for you and pray that the Lord will enable you to get favour and grace from all your authorities as well. I can't just wait to see you to be a blooming doctor in the near future.

Jiji, you are my only sister on the planet now, I cherish your love very much as an older sister. Fortunately, I could impart life values to you in a small way I think. We lovingly call you Jiji after her passing away when you were just six months old. Amma lovingly called you Lucy. You had many of the privileges and also disadvantages being the youngest of the family. You learnt to sing many songs and learnt many memory verses while you were young. You taught yourself to play the harmonium. You have such a melodious voice; and we all used to sing together in our home with our parents at 6 PM for our family prayers. What a warm feeling of being secure in His presence!. Still your singing voice rings in my ears. How can I forget your love for me , that is who you are. Coming to recollect, you used to be easy going and very casual. Unlike me you learnt cycling with friends from the neighbourhood. Papa had relaxed many of his family rules and restrictions for you.

When we as a family visited home for vacation from Abu Dhabi you really took care of us very well. Our children were very fond of you and even their aunty Suji, your older sister. Both of you made those vacations a memorable time of our life. Those were the best time with you both my dear sisters. I had spent longer periods of time with you all, say a month or so during our vacation. Charles, your beloved husband, an automobile engineer, and you eventually moved to Gurgaon near New Delhi. You found a good school where you happily started working. God has blessed you both with two handsome boys, Jickson and Runold. Eventually life had its own changes, twists and turns. You resigned and came back to south India or again.

After having worked in international Schools in Delhi, Jiji, you continued your educational career in Kanniyakumari District and later in Maldives. When Charles came back to Kanniyakumari District from Delhi, he invested his experiences in business. Jiji used to remind me of the education, which our parents gave us even when we do not know what is even best for our future. Yes I am sure this is an imperishable treasure in our entire life, which enabled us to even go abroad and work.

Jickson, you are a very loving, gentle, God fearing boy. I have seen you very much interested in cars and their mechanical, technical aspects even when you were growing up. My wishes for you are that you should keep dreaming and work at it in line with your desires. You must know that 'there is no substitute for hard work'. You are studying presently to be an engineer. With your hard work and wise planning and time management you can reach the top soon to bring laurels to your family. We are behind you to back you up with prayer support. I am very sure you have a bright future. Your prayers and your deep desires will be granted to you in your life. Your dreams and passions are truly going to reward you and come to fulfilment. I can't just wait to see what our Lord has in store for you. May you succeed in each step of you future.

Ronald, I remember you recalling your childhood memories with us at Mount Sinai. You said something like this over the telephone: 'When we visited you during our holidays, we enjoyed exceptional fun times. The event that stood out above everything was the lively family prayer times, when Angel Akka played the organ and Adlien Akka played her violin. Joshua Annan is fun to play with. Thinking of those dinner time with you all; definitely 'a treat' it was. The open ground just outside the house was a treat to run around and play with Josh Annan along with Jicky the dog. When the parting time arrived we kids were given something as a parting gift, which gave us great joy. Once I got a geometry box'.

You are an intelligent gentleman now, and knowing you as a little boy, you love grades growing up and you even obtained centum in your school final exam for Mathematics. Presently you are doing Computer Science Engineering. I think you are interested in programming and software development since you have good analytical and reasoning skills. My wishes and blessings for your bright future. May you bring more innovative and marvellous findings in this field of your choice and dreams.

Here ends the personal notes to my loved ones, who share my blood bond.

VII. *To My Dear Co-Workers And Friends*

How can I forget all my co-workers who laboured with me right from the planting of the Mount Sinai School from the early years of our lives here? Some of you even stayed on through the difficult days of the pandemic until we finally had to close down our work in this village under this unavoidable situation. Your professional help and support are commendable. You all have been teachable and were willing to learn and serve in this village. I vividly recollect the difficulties we encountered, the long hours of hard work, the challenges we faced in spite of selfless work, and opposition from different people even from the community we served. As I come to the end of this book, I want to congratulate and to appreciate you my colleagues.

You stood beside me in this part of the journey of life. The weekend prayer sessions, monthly fasting prayers and devotions in the mornings sustained us through those tough times. The team work with all of you during different sessions like, practicing for the Christmas day program, annual day celebrations and other special events were memorable. Dear friends and co-workers, I say, well done! In the big picture of life we had those great times of working together, learning from each other and growing together. In the eyes of our Lord, all of our hard work was not in vain.

As 1 Corinthians 15:58 says, our hard work is never in vain, rather a reward is waiting for each one of us at the end. Never forget your commendable service and commitment towards those young students. According to Matthew 25:40, Jesus said 'Assuredly, I say to you, inasmuch as you did it to one of the least of these My brethren, you did it to Me.'. Be blessed in all that you continue to do.

CHAPTER FIFTY-TWO

A GENERAL REPORT

It is God who works in you to will and to act in order to fulfil his good purpose.(Philippians 2:13)

A couple of things I would like to mention now. One of them is that I really had a deep desire while joining my college studies, to do a Master's degree in English literature early in my life. Although this desire was denied to me early on in my life, it was fulfilled nearly two decades later after our three children were born. My beloved husband made my dream come true, he encouraged me to enroll in Kamaraj University in Madurai to pursue my Post Graduation through correspondence while I was still working in Abu Dhabi.

Now, regarding my one other dream to become a medical doctor to serve the community, it did happen although this desire did not come to be fulfilled the way I dreamt of. He knows the best for me, Who am I to question our God? Strange enough, five decades later when I was at the end stage of serving in this village, I was awarded a doctorate degree on 15 March 2015 as Doctor of philosophy (Biblical Studies) by the University of Jerusalem. This degree was awarded considering the calibre and credibility of my service and my work in this village. Not a medical degree, though.

About me, at last I am overwhelmed with all my life events, pondering over them all one by one. I think I have already had a blessed life even though there were hardships and questions and pains with uncertainties with untimely deaths and loss all along life's journey. Imagining my life as a train, I started from my knowledgeable young age as the starting point of my journey. I see all along passengers getting on and getting off. There are heavy and light luggage. I understand the heavier the luggage, the more difficult the journey becomes. When our destination comes, we get off and the remaining passengers keep journeying on. When at one point all the passengers are out of the train the journey ends finally.

Epilogue

There have been many puzzling situations and scary curves, cliffs, valleys and plains. I never met anyone who has gone the very same path as mine - so different, and no one knows where and when I started, where the journey came from and where I am going to. It had been a narrow path, steep and winding but only one step ahead of me at a time. I have witnessed at least four generations of people gone before me: my grandparents, uncles, aunts, father and mother, my sisters and brothers, my friends, young children and babies.

How long I will live on this earth, I do not know but what I do know is that He has my reins in His hand and He knows when my life ends here. That's when all my pains and tears will also end. But I know this thing of myself, I was a sinner but I am washed and cleansed by the precious blood of the only Saviour and my Lord Jesus Christ.

The constant reminder of my Lord is that He has not left me alone for a moment all my life. When I asked for forgiveness of my sins, that moment He not only forgave me my past, but also gave me hope for the future and became my Saviour all through eternity.

There is really nothing that one could do that would last for long or accomplish as much really as sharing God and His love with others. And it is not really that hard if you make a conscious effort to do it. So many people around us need God's love. We need to use our mouth, our hands and our feet and heart. We need God to move through us.

The last and the best step of life is to walk into God's arms. It will be the culmination of a long journey. The last step will be the best step. God will be there to meet and greet me, embrace me and welcome me into heaven. Then we will experience the total peace and joy together with him. So I look forward to that moment.

As we age physically, our bodies are just tired from the wear and tear of life. Our heart is tired from pumping day and night, our muscles are tired from all the movements, our nerves are tired from mental strain; and on and on it goes. But if we do not feel so tired and do not have all the aches and pains, we may not wish to leave our body behind and get ready to go home to heaven. This is one way God is preparing us all to move on.

These are the years when the strength; and flesh fades into the background so the strength of the spirit can flourish and grow. This is a special time for me to reflect and meditate, a time that is no longer crowded out by current demands. Having this special time together with my Lord my Creator is indeed a reward. While I am lamenting the tiredness and the weakening of my frame, I see beyond that and see the beauty of how my spirit is drawn closer to the Lord. As life slows down, I am able to speak to my Lord clearly. The Lord wants to answer my questions and heal my hurts. These times are part of God's plan to prepare me for the next life.

As we live in faith, it will have a great effect on others. Long after you are home in heaven, your faith will carry on in others' lives too. Our love for God and His love for us will be the reference points. You will be remembered as a person of faith, someone who trusted God and imparted a peaceful, gentle, loving spirit to everyone around you. The scripture says, 'as a person thinks, so is he.' If we make a habit of viewing situations positively, we will not only be happier for it but we will be a positive person, the kind others love to be around. We know that we cannot take our material possessions with us when we graduate to the next life, but we can take the wisdom and experience we have gained in this life. What you have learned on earth, I believe, will still be used in Heaven.

The way the world is going now, there is a greater need for prayer than ever before. However, the size of God's army of prayer warriors appears to be shrinking. It is heart-breaking to see how many situations are not being helped because very few seem to pray. God has power to do anything, but prayers of His people are needed to activate the power. Meanwhile the lost children wander as sheep with no shepherd because no one pleads their case.

Also those who labour for God could accomplish so much more with prayer power behind them. Can we become prayer warriors? Can we pray consistently and fervently? There are thousands whom we could help through prayer. Rise to the challenge and you can help change someone's world. We may change the course of history from our humble corner. This ministry of prayer could be our crowning achievement.

I truly understand it's difficult sometimes to accept help. Even when you're very weak or sick and know you need help, it can also be difficult to trust others. We may think that you know what is best and sometimes you do, but not always. You may be older and wiser in some ways, but it pays to listen to others. Let our loved ones do what they can to make life easier for us. It is one way they show their love. It is a touch of God's love for us. When God puts people in our lives to help us, graciously accept their love.

There is none who is perfect. Do not feel bad about the mistakes you have committed. Is there anyone who has not made mistakes? No, the scripture says 'All have sinned and fallen short of the glory of God' Romans 3;23. But God never looks at your faults and failures. God looks at the heart. Sure there were times we could have done better but He never condemns us. He says, I see a heart that has been trying, in its own special way, to give what it could to God. If our hope is waning, God wants to restore it.

Let us draw closer and closer to God. This is the reward for us who love God. We will find that as years pass by we come closer and closer to God. We will become sweeter and sweeter and more loving. We will find more and more peace inside our spirit. We will be at rest. We can find our soul drawing near to heaven as we look ahead to the glories that await us there. And as we look toward the horizon, toward the blessing of knowing God's love in its completeness in heaven, knowing that God will always delight with us in this life, then when the time comes we will cross the river together, with God holding our hand until we step unto the golden shore on the other side.

Oh, what a rejoicing there will be, when we reach this side, which is our heavenly dwelling place. We will have many rewards waiting for us there. But the days before we go will also be beautiful. The Lord wants us to rest in His arms. We can walk together with him day after day. He stays closer and closer until that final day when we walk no more apart but close as breath to breath, and we know God as God as intimately I know.

God will always come to your rescue. He may not always spare us from problems but will pull us through and give strength to carry on. This is the type of strength He wants to show others through us. We will come to this realm in His time. When our work on earth is finished, this is one of the special rewards He gives to those who love Him. We can know that He will bring us to Him at the perfect time- no sooner and no later.

He sees our struggles and hears our cry for help. When we feel all alone, He is there. He feels our heartaches and waits for us to go to Him in prayer. Let's come into His sanctuary, into the place that you and I can share. There He is able to lift the worries, the cares and the confusion. There He can restore us and infuse us with strength to go on. Life can be a struggle, but we do not have to struggle alone. Many times, God has placed a burden in your life that seems like mountains. They weigh our spirit down and we wonder why? God has done this to bring us closer to Him. He knows our heart better than anyone else ever could; and loves us more dearly.

The problems and obstacles that He has allowed in our life can be taken in two ways. They can make you either bitter or better. God can use us as an instrument of His love to comfort others only when we find peace in Him.

Many things in life may seem unfair and unloving, but when we look at them through the promise in His word saying 'all things work together for good' that gives a whole new meaning to life. That promise holds the key to any heartache, any problem or any fear. He loves us as His own child and always will. We always have a special place in His heart that no one else can ever fill.

Testimony Of A Former Student

Greetings in the name of our Lord and Saviour Jesus Christ. I consider this as an opportunity and honour to write a few words about this book 'Why Me Lord' by Dr Mrs Annie David. I strongly believe that this book will enrich the focus of those seeking counsel to promote His kingdom in their lives.

The amazing love of God to the long forgotten village, where I hail from, stands out among many miracles in my life. The story of how the author received and heeded the divine call while she was still in Abu Dhabi UAE two decades ago, and how her family envisioned coming to our village with a deep desire to reach out to this village. Primarily with imparting education as their goal, they started a primary School against many hindrances. As a little boy of 12 years I desired to be a part of the school they have started. Eventually, I was fortunate enough to join the Spoken English Classes the author conducted for the village youth, adults and others.

I personally knew her family and their passion and commitment for this village. I am indeed drawn to the extravagance of God's love manifested through this family, which helped replace years of darkness prevailed here with His light.

Eventually I accepted he Lord as my Saviour, studied to be an engineer and started my carrier as a Technical Assistant in ISRO. Since the love of God persuaded me to follow God's calling for ministry, I have joined the Bible College and I am equipped to be His servant in this very village.

I have been blessed by Dr Annie's continued counsel and other help as well. I am sure there are many more persons in this village and around who are blessed by their work in this village. Thanking the Lord for sending you, Dr Annie, and your dear family to our village; and even your willingness to be a part of us in this village.

May the Lord encourage many others from here, too, to do the work of the Lord here as you have sown the seeds in their lives, too. As the scripture says, 'Harvest is plenty and the labourers are few'. I desire many people will not only read this fabulous book, but also heed His call as it is very distinctly portrayed in this awesome book.

Blessings,
Pastor Manex Deepa Prabhu, DME, BTh.,
Vishnupuram Colony, Erachakulam,

Kanniyakumari District

Afterword 1

It gives me immense pleasure and I deem it a privilege to write a few words about this book, 'Why me Lord', by Dr. Mrs. Annie Isabel David. I am sure that reading this book will edify you for a Godly life, encourage you to do good works prudently, and empower you to be successful.

May God strengthen your inner man, shape your mind and specialise your life to do and to see great things in the days to come. The Lord reminds me of the verse in Zechariah 4:10, Who can despise a small beginning? May our Good Lord glorify Annie to write even greater things in the days to come (John 1.50).

Dear reader, as you begin reading this book, may God make you, mould you and magnify you when you pass through trials, tests and temptations and transform you into a living testimony as expressed by the author. I pray and hope that you will not miss the essence and the core message of this book.

Pastor Caleb Jeyakumar,
Bethel Mission Church,
Kattathurai, Kanniyakumari District

Afterword 2

I am indeed thrilled to add my tribute to my sister Annie David's book titled 'Why Me Lord'. I am deeply impressed and inspired by this book, which compels each one to see beyond now and to invest for His kingdom. I have watched and experienced her selfless love for the Lord and her obedience and dedication to Jesus, who is the author and perfecter of our faith.

From my childhood I have experienced Annie's unique love and concern for me, which is very special and it's something like that of a mother's love. The care she has given me was more than of a sister. I recollect even when I was at the primary school that she helped me with my school lessons. The vivid picture of her sitting beside me to help me with the homework, coached me with my school lessons even to the point of making me memorize the poems, tables in Maths and so on.

The outstanding memories even now and I am proud of my sister, were about her teaching me consonants and vowels and the intricate supporting symbols of Tamil letters. She adopted a systematic teaching style using sound analogy method, whereby I could write and read Tamil confidently without mistakes in front of my class.

Interestingly even the brilliant students tend to make mistakes in pronouncing and writing the letters. In fact this has been one of her great investments in my life. Apart from school studies my sister also trained me to read my Bible and also memorise the scripture verses.

The one other area where she had influenced me, which I could never forget, was the many singing sessions she had given me during my high school days. With her list selected songs in advance, she eventually prepared me for singing competitions both at church and in my school.

The trouble she took to teach the lyrics and to train me for singing was well rewarded. In fact I have bagged the first prizes almost in all the competitions. Recollecting now, a particular song, which she trained me for the competition, readily captured the hearts and ears of the judges of the competition, even my teachers at school. As a result, they would keep asking me to sing the same song for them over and over again on several occasions.

Growing up, even while I was in Medical college she had invested in me financially when I needed it the most; for which I continue to remain grateful. Even when she went to Abu Dhabi she thought of me and sent me a gift package through a student who visited his parents in Abu Dhabi during his vacation, which included a pair of Nike shoes. I was very proud of wearing them and thank her for her sweet gesture.

The best gift she could ever give me, like a cherry on top of the cream of the cake, was the eighty base red coloured Yamaha piano accordion. I had the pleasant memory of opening the accordion myself and try to figure out how to start playing. Later years I improved, in turn revolutionizing my musical lifestyle with the latest version of an accordion. Today I am able to play for different music directors in different places for God's glory and for His kingdom work.

May God bless this book for which she worked very hard over the years. Even as the readers, takes time to understand the work of our God through this book, to be transformed in each one of our lives.

Dr. W.H. Isaac Sunder Sen,
M.S., M.C.H., D.N.B. (Ortho)
Fellow Joint Replacement (Germany & U.K.)
Fellow AO Spine, Hip & knee and spine surgery, Marthandam

Afterword 3

The privilege to write an afterword to the book 'Why me Lord?' authored by Dr. Annie David, came as a pleasant surprise to me. Having read through the book, I feel I am really privileged, though unworthy, to write here.

The book is a narration of the real life experience of the author in a simple language so that anyone who reads it will understand the author's purpose. Her childhood lifestyle enabled her to cling on to her faith in the Lord Jesus even when she went through hardships, sickness and disappointments.

The thread which runs through is the author's love for the Lord and her determination to maintain it till the last. She has beautifully intertwined the cultural setting of the time in which she grew up. Throughout the book the author has brought out the deepest personal relationship with the Lord Jesus Christ.

I am greatly challenged and inspired by reading through the book and I wish it will be a source of inspiration to every reader.

John Mathew B.Th.,
Bagayam, CMC College Campus, Vellore.

Afterword 4

I am privileged to write an afterword for the book entitled 'Why Me Lord' which is an autobiography of my elder sister Dr. Annie David. When I turned each page of the book, I was taken aback by the cherishing memories of the 1970s and 80s that we lived in our ancestral home in Paloor, which is located in Vilavancode Taluk of Kanniyakumari district.

The book portrays various life and family events of the author covering five generations, and tries to reconstruct events related to our maternal as well as paternal grandparents, including the settings of the author's grandchildren. She attempts to connect her faith through examples of various life events to reassure the hope, peace, joy, love and fulfilment of life.

The author is a versatile personality and has diverse talents with qualifications in various academic disciplines. She worked as a teacher of Science as well as a physical educator in various higher institutions both in India and abroad. She possesses good leadership qualities, kind heart, and readiness to extend a helping hand to poor and needy people. Not only was she kind to human beings but also with animals. I remember, once our mother told us that when she was young she shared her food even to stray dogs and sometimes brought them home. She was also efficient in painting, stitching, embroidery and music. Moreover, she has passed on all her talents to her children.

Being the last sibling and a late child to my parents, I was much pampered by everyone in the family. Even my sister extended her motherly love and care towards me during my early childhood, which remains ever fresh in my mind but I did not get much privilege to be with her for a long time as she moved to Abu Dhabi when I began middle school. She spent quality time with us all during her visits to India for vacation.

This book is her great contribution not only for our family and this generation, but also for the generations to come. It presents my sister's life events, the hardships she faced, narrating the events in a vivid manner to demonstrate how she sought the face of God in times of darkness and how she is being protected by God throughout her life's journey. This book will definitely enlighten the readers and help them to revive their faith and stand steadfast in their calling. The book will also provide the readers a glimpse of the past lifestyle of the western Kanniyakumari district as well as contemporary life of that region as it covers five generations of our family. Hence, it can be a great resource of information for the readers who are curious about the past history and culture of the area. Apart from this, this book will certainly be a reference for the members of our family; and I am sure the forthcoming generation will keep adding details in the future.

I wish her good health and eternal blessings. May the blessings she passes on to the following generations come true. Let her literary efforts be continued and bring blessings to many. Let His name be glorified!

W.H. Jiji Malar Christabel M.Sc., M.Ed.,
Teacher, Ministry of Education,
The Republic of Maldives.

Afterword 5

It is an immense honour and privilege to write this as I reflect on this wonderful labour of love that my dear mother has been writing. I have been so blessed to witness as her daughter the love and the passion she has for the Lord and to be raised in the fear of God and love for Him and what matters in the light of eternity even as I saw my precious mother do the same on a daily basis.

Memories of my early moments at home are vividly punctuated with seeing my parents seek God and His word at the beginning of the day as well as their call for us to also reflect as a family in the morning and in the evening and several times in between. Amma took the time to spend one on one time with me and teach me from a very young age of the matters of life which I should be cautious about and always pointed me back to the Lord and His will. Perhaps one of my greatest lessons from Amma is that we have one life the one that Jesus gave us, and that living to honour Him in everything I ever did in life is all that really matters.

Whilst I have had the privilege to see the example of a godly mother in my mother even as a child, she has been my best friend, and someone I always look up to even now. In her own life, my mother has gone through her own path of unique walk with the Lord where she has surrendered even the difficult moments to the Lord and trusted Him to see her through. As she depends on the Lord for each and every thing, I have seen the way the Lord has led her and all of us and it has been marvellous to witness.

In this book, as you read it, you will also have the chance to see glimpses of loss, release, gain, questions and answers, adventures, different seasons and stages of life; but through it all, there is the golden thread of God's sovereign hand intertwined in the pages of this book.

When I look back at the 33 years of life I have had the chance to do life alongside my dear mother, across miles when we were in different countries, as well as the past few years when we worked together in the school and even watching her journey as she painstakingly put in the effort into this book, I pray that you may be aware of the Saviour's love for you as well. I pray that you too may embark on your own journey of faith and love as you walk with Jesus every day in His perfect love.

- Angelina Esther David, M.A., M.B.A.
Clinical Psychologist. PLUMM Health, U.K.

Pictures

Me with my parents (1956)

Me at Duthie School (1969)

Lucas family (2001)

Koshy, Angelina, Avidan, Zuriel and Liam

Toby, Adlien, Caleb and Amaeya

Joshua and Grasia

Lucas Family (2022)